GARDENING INDOORS UNDER LIGHTS

FREDERICK H. KRANZ

and

JACQUELINE L. KRANZ

FOREWORD BY R. J. DOWNS

Gardening Indoors under Lights

NEW REVISED EDITION

New York / THE VIKING PRESS

First published in 1957 by The Viking Press, Inc.
625 Madison Avenue, New York, N.Y. 10022

Published in Canada by
The Macmillan Company of Canada Limited

Revised edition issued in 1971

SBN 670-33489-8

Library of Congress catalog card number: 70-124323

Printed in U.S.A.

Fifth printing January 1975

FOREWORD

Probably the first attempt to use artificial light for growing plants was made by L. H. Bailey in 1893. The light source was a carbon arc lamp, enclosed in glass to absorb the damaging ultraviolet radiation. The results showed that electric light could be used to advantage for plant growth, and Bailey called the new technique electro-horticulture.

Although a few other investigators experimented with carbon arc and with incandescent-filament lamps, the use of artificial light for plant growth did not receive much attention until about fifty years ago. It was in 1920 that W. W. Garner and H. A. Allard discovered that photoperiod, or length of day, controlled the flowering of many kinds of plants.

Use of artificial light to control day-length soon became a tool for biological research and for commercial plant production. The United States Department of Agriculture set up a special photoperiod project in Beltsville, Maryland, to increase our ability to use the new tool and to learn how plants measured the relative lengths of the day and night. This project, headed by H. A. Borthwick with the cooperation of S. B. Hendricks, became a Pioneering Research Group in Plant Physiology and gained international fame as the "Beltsville Group." This research team discovered the pigment phytochrome by which plants absorb the photoperiod controlling light and by which the plants measure time.

As might be expected, it was only a step from the use of artificial light for controlling photoperiod in greenhouses to growing plants in completely artificially lighted rooms. Some of the earliest of these rooms were built at Beltsville using carbon arc and incandescent lamps, and a great deal of information was gained as scientists awaited the development of the more suitable fluorescent light source. As early as 1940 A. W. Naylor examined the kind of plant growth obtained under fluorescent lamps, and large rooms completely lighted by fluorescent lamps were in operation at the California Institute of Technology phytotron by 1950.

The Cal Tech phytotron has been permanently shut down and the United States Department of Agriculture has seen fit to disband the "Beltsville Group." Work toward better plant growth under artificial lights in controlled environments continues, however, at the Phytoengineering Laboratory at Beltsville, at the North Carolina State University phytotron, and at numerous other colleges and universities. In general, the research of the past and present has not been aimed at helping the hobbyist and homeowner. Although the fluorescent lamp has made possible electro-horticulture in the home—Frederick and Jacqueline Kranz have made it practical.

R. J. Downs, Director
Phytotron
North Carolina State University

PREFACE

The story of one of our great recent discoveries has been unfolding before us almost unnoticed: man's ability to duplicate indoors the radiant energy of the sun.

Over the past few years people have, almost incredulously, watched amateurs growing plants indoors under lights. They may have noticed that in March florists sell chrysanthemums as beautiful as those that bloom in November. They may have read that scientific research in the life-sciences has postponed the food shortage. They may even have heard of phytotrons, the laboratories under artificial lights, where all the conditions that help or hinder a plant's growth can be studied and where scientists can simulate the environment of the temperate zone, of the tropics, and of the far north. The purpose of this book is to tell something of the history of this remarkable discovery and to provide information about the practical means by which the scientist, the student, and the amateur can continue to explore its applications.

In the 1940s when my husband and I began growing plants indoors under a combination of fluorescent and incandescent lamps, most people had never heard of such a thing. Since then thousands of amateurs have grown plants under lights.

The results of our research during the 1940s and 1950s were published in *Gardening Indoors under Lights*. But the research did not stop after the book appeared. We continued to fill notebook after notebook until we felt that so many new discoveries needed telling that the original book should be revised. This seems to be the pattern of those investigating the use of radiant energy indoors. The Earhart Phytotron of the California Institute of Technology, before it closed permanently, would shut down every five years just to catch up regularly with the new discoveries being made there.

Just as the revision was in full swing, Frederick Kranz passed away. He was a scientist of distinction, a director of chemical research by profession, and a dedicated grower of plants by avocation. He used the training of a lifetime of research to solve the special problems of growing plants under lights in the home. Rarely do amateurs have the benefit of such careful work. He took nothing for granted. His habit of noticing the smallest detail and explaining procedures clearly and thoroughly made *Gardening Indoors under Lights* literally a bible to those who love plants. This book includes both his original research and the new work that he recorded so carefully.

Professionals and amateurs who wish to grow plants under lights for pleasure or profit will find the pages of this book filled with new and helpful material. Teachers and students in universities and high schools will find here hard-to-obtain information on recent scientific advances in the field, together with a number of experiments that can easily be carried out at home or in the classroom. It is my hope that the book will also be of interest to the general reader who wishes to read the fascinating story of a great discovery whose future importance is only now beginning to be realized.

My great appreciation is due Dr. R. J. Downs, director of the phytotron of North Carolina State University, for his help in reading the manuscript and clarifying certain sections. Special thanks are also due to the many who have helped me in collecting information and to those whose work has pioneered the way for us to follow, especially Dr. H. A. Borthwick, A. A. Piringer of the National Arboretum, Henry M. Cathey, J. M. Buck, and Chris C. Mpelkas. I am also particularly grateful to Walter Kranz, who is such a great gardener, and to Cornelia J. Haley for her great help in the most intangible ways.

JACQUELINE L. KRANZ

CONTENTS

~ ix

ILLUSTRATIONS

Tomatoes blossoming under lights
Plants growing on a four-tier stand
Fixture combining incandescent and fluorescent light
Incandescent lights added to Gro-Lux tube
Completely enclosed lamplight greenhouse
Temperature plays an important part in growth
Propagating box and rooted cuttings growing in soil
Chinese cabbage and other vegetables growing under lights
An unused niche in the basement transformed
into propagating area

FOLLOWING PAGE   148

Flowers in your window garden
African violets grown under different light intensities
Effect of light on germination and growth
Phytotron at North Carolina State University
The effect of carbon dioxide on plant growth
Two types of lamps
Floraliter tray
Lights over a simple bench
Orchids and African violets
Floribunda rose, Chatter
Vegetables with automatic watering

PART I

The Great Discoveries

GARDENING

BY LAMPLIGHT

Gardening by lamplight was a revolutionary idea. Its principles, first developed in the 1920s, have completely changed agricultural and horticultural concepts. It has pointed the way toward feeding a hungry world. Through research made possible by this discovery, farmers have learned the varieties of wheat they must plant in various latitudes so that their crops may develop enough to produce seed. Florists have learned to control the blossoming-time of plants. Nature's long-kept secret of why crocuses bloom in the spring and chrysanthemums in the fall, of why apples turn red and leaves change colors has been revealed.

In this century, our knowledge has increased so rapidly that we accept the breaking of age-old limits as the natural order of things, almost as a commonplace. But only when you are a part of these discoveries—if simply by enabling a flower to blossom in a dark corner of your house without benefit of daylight—do you know of a surety it is no commonplace. You feel the full impact of discovery. You share the excitement with plant researchers, scientists, and horticulturists by growing plants in a controlled environment.

The home gardener can make practical use of this great scientific breakthrough. Rarely does an individual have such an opportunity.

Instead of seeing experiments on television or reading about them in newspapers, you can test these principles in your own living room. It is merely a matter of scale. Elaborate growth-control rooms, called phytotrons, can produce a light intensity measuring half the intensity of sunlight. Yet it is possible to grow flowers in the home with two coolwhite fluorescent tubes and one 25-watt incandescent bulb. In fact, you can regenerate your plants by using just one 60-watt incandescent bulb.

Plants can be grown in the home under lights as they have never been grown before. Roses will bloom indoors—not just in June, but the whole year through. African violets can reach a foot in diameter and have two hundred blossoms open, and the lady's-slipper orchid, the *Cypripedium*, can blossom—as it did for us—on its first growth.

With the proper use of artificial lights you can start your tomatoes, broccoli, cucumbers—in fact all your vegetables—indoors and have stockier plants than you can get from professional growers by the time you are ready to plant them in your garden.

Until the discovery was made that plants could be grown as well under artificial lights as in sunshine, light was the variable that interfered with truly scientific research. Today it is possible for scientists in phytotrons to control and adjust all the conditions affecting plant growth.

The work that is done under these conditions produces such incredible results that the home gardener is apt to be intimidated and turn away from the principles laid down by professionals, feeling that his home—with dogs and cats and children—is a long way from being a controlled environment. But it is possible to develop garden spots in your home where you can achieve varying degrees of control. Thousands of amateurs have demonstrated this to their own satisfaction.

Long before we began experimenting with artificial light, we had been convinced that light, temperature, and soil were the most important factors in plant growth. But we had not made much progress in proving it. Some winters our windows would be filled with staghorn ferns and blossoming begonias, and our friends would exclaim, "How do you do it? We can't make anything grow." The next winter this situation would be reversed, and nothing would grow for us. It was rather baffling.

The whole picture was changed when we discovered how well plants would grow under artificial light. We began in the early 1940s with a 60-watt bulb. There were no guidelines, but in just two weeks the effect on our struggling houseplants seemed to us miraculous. Many amateurs have since experienced this wonder, but for us it had far-reaching results. Until that time, it had taken a whole winter to grow an experimental plant on a windowsill, and such slow growth made results inconclusive; but, with all plants growing as rapidly as those we had placed under the 60-watt bulb, changes in growing conditions could be accurately gauged. Laboratory conditions, as we wanted them, could be created right in our own home.

The basement became a place devoted to experimental study. Various growth areas were established. Lights were put in the fruit cellar, which was cool. The tool bench and the old dresser were equipped with various combinations of fluorescent tubes and incandescent bulbs. We also built a completely enclosed case where plants could be grown in a controlled atmosphere. The rapid growth of the plants made it imperative for us to provide more and more space for them. At the height of our work, we had six different types of "indoor greenhouses" in the basement, with several extensions upstairs. Thousands of plants were grown under slightly differing conditions, and each of these had its own card and case history.

At first we deliberately worked with low light intensities so that our results could be duplicated by other gardeners who had neither the time nor the means for elaborate light arrangements. As new lights were developed, we worked with somewhat higher light intensities, yet the light intensity in our most successful case was only 1500 foot-candles, an intensity easily available to any amateur. Although plants would grow under almost any lamp, there were certain combinations and arrangements under which they would grow as perfectly as in commercial glass-covered greenhouses. Actually, they grew even better—but no one believed us when we said so. We found that the proper lights, combined with the right soil, water, temperature, and atmospheric conditions, could make *any* plant flourish like the proverbial green bay tree.

Everyone who came into our home rushed with us to the basement to stand spellbound before cases of orchids, African violets, begonias, and roses—all flourishing as if they were being grown out of doors. When we exhibited some of these plants at the International Flower Show in New York, some very knowledgeable judges could not believe that they had been grown exclusively under lights.

Today gardening by lamplight still has the aura of discovery, although it also has received the accolade of full acceptance. Mail-order houses are offering small assemblages to anyone who wants to try his hand. Manufacturers advertise lamps designed especially for the indoor gardener's use, and no one raises an eyebrow when someone points out that a particularly beautiful plant has been grown without natural light.

The discovery has been put into use in some surprising ways. Two scientists made a garden grow twenty feet under polar ice, a mere eight hundred yards from the South Pole,* with the help of an incandescent bulb and a fluorescent tube. Dwarf marigolds blossomed, onions and carrots sprouted, and parsley was harvested and chopped to garnish soup.

Thousands of feet under the sea in a Polaris submarine, fresh vegetables and greens have been grown continuously under fluorescent tubes.

Even in the extensive tests made at the Lunar Receiving Laboratory in Houston after the Apollo 11 flight, gardening indoors under lights played a part.† Botanists looking for harmful effects to earthly life found, instead, a benefit. An exotic lunar vitamin speeded a liverwort's growth by 300 per cent, ferns thrived on it, and even the homely lettuce found it nourishing. And how were these experiments carried out? Under lights. Dr. Charles Walkinshaw's group used thirty-three types of plants for testing. Light for growing plants has ceased to be a wonder and has become an accepted tool.

You will find, as we did, that there are always new plants to try, new wonders to behold. Like any new technique, gardening by artificial light has its problems. The failures add spice to the victories and help to induce humility in the bumptious indoor gardener who, after years of mediocrity, suddenly finds himself a startling success.

The guidelines suggested in this book are not just pet theories or

* *The New York Times*, December 4, 1962.
† *The Christian Science Monitor*, November 21, 1969.

hearsay advice, but the results of thousands of experiments carried out entirely in our home under conditions you can duplicate. The materials you need are right at hand and inexpensive. You will find the proverbial "green thumb" that every gardener longs to possess becoming, through the pages of this book, "rule of thumb."

INDOOR SUNLIGHT

We might as well plunge immediately into the secret that has made lamplight gardening possible. By combining fluorescent tubes and incandescent bulbs in the ratio of 3 watts of fluorescent to 1 watt of incandescent you can produce excellent growing conditions for plants. Scientists refer to this combination as "balanced lighting." Astounding as it seems, this formula enables you to bypass the sun.

The scientific explanation of this phenomenon is best understood by thinking of a prism as it divides the rays of light into distinct rainbow colors. These colored rays make up what is known as the visible spectrum. Light rays that are not seen by the human eye are referred to as the invisible, or infra-red, spectrum. All of the visible rays and at least one in the invisible spectrum are known to affect the growth of plants to some extent. The vital rays are the blue at 450 nanometer units, the red at 650 nanometer units, and the far-red at 730 nanometer units. (The nanometer—nm—is the currently accepted unit for measuring the length of light waves. A nanometer is one millionth of a millimeter or 254 ten-millionths of an inch. Scientists express it in writing as 10^{-9} meters.) The blue and red rays are in the visible spectrum, the far-red in the first stage of the invisible spectrum, known as the near-visible spectrum.

Fortunately for the home gardener, two kinds of lamps commonly used in the home produce these rays and are easily adapted for growing plants. Fluorescent tubes produce blue and red rays, and the incandescent filament bulb emits the red and far-red rays. When combined in the proper ratio, these lamps can create the conditions that make plant growth possible. Although plants can be grown for considerable periods of time under either a fluorescent tube or an incandescent bulb, the health of the plants and the abundance of flowers are increased when they are given balanced lighting. When only one of these types of lamps is being used, you can, of course, obtain balanced lighting by placing the lamp by a window. The natural light supplies the necessary rays and the artificial lamps increase the light intensity so that the plants will grow much more rapidly.

One of the earliest experimental research centers was in the growth-control rooms of the United States Department of Agriculture at Beltsville, Maryland. During the 1920s, under a mighty battery of incandescent bulbs and fluorescent tubes, a crop of soybeans was grown simultaneously with a crop in the field, and the results made history. The beans grown out of doors could not be distinguished from those grown under artificial lights! During the course of this research, it was determined that the blue light promoted foliage growth and that red rays encouraged flowering. This is an important point to remember and one that you can apply immediately to your own indoor gardening.

The significance of these rays was understood early in the development of this light science, but the importance of the far-red ray in the near-visible spectrum was not realized until early in the 1960s, as a result of the discovery of phytochrome, a light-sensitive pigment common to all growing plants.* The government team of scientists, headed by Dr. H. A. Borthwick, found that this "Dr. Jekyll and Mr. Hyde" enzyme rapidly changes form when exposed to minutely differing wave lengths of red and far-red light. These changes serve to operate "nature's clock," which regulates such diverse phenomena as shrubs ceasing to grow in the fall, leaves turning red and yellow, and apples acquiring a rosy blush on one side but not on the other. It ap-

---

* See *Scientific American*, September 1962, for an account of this discovery written by Dr. R. J. Downs and Dr. Butler.

pears that phytochrome controls the timing of a plant's life—from the sprouting of a seed to the flowering of the plant, including even the dormancy period.

As soon as the influence of the far-red rays on phytochrome was demonstrated, attention was focused on the incandescent bulb, which had been less popular with hobbyists because of the heat it produces. Some indoor gardeners had found it easier to use fluorescent tubes alone, contenting themselves with fewer flowers, or to use phosphor lamps, fluorescent tubes specially altered in order to increase the output of the red and blue rays. It is now clear, however, that these substitutes do not solve the problem of achieving completely balanced lighting, since they fail to provide the far-red rays. While fluorescent light is also needed, we believe that the most practical source of far-red rays for the home gardener is still the incandescent bulb, and in Chapter 3 we will discuss several simple ways to reduce the effects of the heat produced by this bulb so that high light intensity can be obtained without scorching the plants.

Dr. R. J. Downs, who was a member of the team that discovered phytochrome, points out, however, that the source or amount of light is not nearly as important as the *ratio* of far-red to red rays. We have successfully used the formula of 30 watts of incandescent light to 100 watts of fluorescent for over twenty years and it is still the ratio to use if you are working with comparatively low light intensities—from 250 foot-candles to 1000 foot-candles. Recent studies show that as the illuminance, or light intensity, increases, the percentage of incandescent light must be increased. In some installations where there is very high illuminance from Power-Groove tubes, the ratio is 50 watts of incandescent to 100 watts of fluorescent light. In most home installations, where the degree of illuminance is between 1200 and 2000 foot-candles, however, the ideal ratio is 35 or 40 watts of incandescent to 100 of fluorescent light. There it is: the formula for artificial sunlight. Our forefathers would never have believed it existed. It is awe-inspiring even to most of us nowadays!

In figuring the number of incandescent bulbs you will need to use with your fluorescent tubes to give balanced lighting, you may be tempted to ignore the incandescent bulbs because their number seems so small. Do not do it. If your objective is to have plants that flower abundantly, it is well worth the trouble to install the required number of incandescent bulbs. You may find it necessary to use bulbs having slightly more watts than the formula demands, because incandescent bulbs are not manufactured in the exact sizes corresponding to fluorescent tubes. As long as the deviation from the formula does not mean fewer watts, the difference is not important.

Balanced lighting, however it is achieved, may be likened to conditions in the sunny borders of our gardens, where flowers blossom and vegetation runs riot. When only fluorescent tubes or only incandescent bulbs are used, the environment that either creates is similar to the shady borders of our gardens. We ourselves may enjoy both sun and shade, but we must adapt our plants to the environment in which they will grow best.

If you wish to grow only foliage plants, you can use either cool-white fluorescent lamps or incandescent bulbs alone. Fluorescent tubes and phosphor lamps are usually preferred to incandescent bulbs because the plants can grow within four inches of a tube—or even closer—without being burned, so that high light intensities may be obtained.

It is also true that plants grown under fluorescent lights alone do not show the deficiency in their light diet as quickly nor to so marked a degree as they do under incandescent lamps. The deficiency is most apparent in the lack of flowers. For some time, we had only fluorescent lamps in one of the lamplight greenhouses. The African violets, the shrimp plant, and especially the begonia, flowered quite sparsely. We added the needed red and far-red light—in this case it amounted to only three 40-watt incandescent bulbs. Within three to five weeks the difference was so astounding that it made us devotees of balanced lighting wherever we could possibly obtain it. The begonias were the most surprising. The semperflorens, which had had no flowers at all, began to blossom at every leaf axil; the Arthur Mallot begonia, which had produced only a few scattered blossoms, burst into full bloom, and the flowers on the African violets more than doubled.

We have grown all types of foliage plants under incandescent bulbs. Among them are the branching ivy, the strawberry geranium, the grape ivy (sometimes called the vitis), the Boston fern, the piggyback plant, the holly fern, the peperomia, the African evergreen, and the hoya. Eventually the effect of the lopsided diet the plants are getting under these lights becomes apparent. Even the peperomia, which survives the longest, gradually develops thin stems and long distances between the leaf nodes. The plants recuperate, however, if placed under balanced lighting for a season.

A very simple experiment will illustrate graphically the relative effects of incandescent bulbs, fluorescent tubes, and the natural light coming through most windowpanes *in winter*. (Light conditions are, of course, quite different in spring, summer, and early fall.) We used several different plants for the experiment, but you can settle for one variety if you prefer. Buy three grape ivy plants or root three cuttings in separate pots. Place one pot on the windowsill, another under an incandescent bulb, and the third under a fluorescent tube. Within two weeks you will be able to see some changes in both plants under the lights, but the one on the windowsill will look just about as it did when you placed it there.

At the end of six weeks the plant under the fluorescent lamp will have outgrown the others, and the one under the incandescent bulb will be a close second. The plant whose fortunes depended on natural light will be a very poor third.

In our experiment the results were spectacular. The plants under both types of light had deep green leaves and bushy stems. The main stem of the plant under the fluorescent lamp was twenty-one inches tall; that of the plant under the incandescent bulb had reached a height of seventeen inches; but the poor windowsill plant had only one and a half inches of growth to its credit.

FACTS ABOUT LIGHTS

Today indoor gardeners and amateur experimenters have many advantages over those who began gardening under lights some twenty years ago. Plant physiologists have sought out the best types of lamps available for plant growth. Lamp manufacturers have done much research to develop lamps specifically adapted for use with plants. There is also the experience of many lamplight gardeners to draw upon. You can now select from a wide variety of lamps the ones that are best for your purpose.

It is a good idea to have an elementary knowledge of the technical properties of incandescent bulbs and fluorescent lamps in order to mount and use them intelligently. Both types of lighting are so familiar that it is easy to overlook certain features that will affect your success in bringing the sun indoors.

❋ The Fluorescent Lamp

High light intensity is essential to the process of photosynthesis, the process by which plants grow, and this is supplied in abundance by the fluorescent lamp. Fundamentally, a fluorescent lamp consists of a coated glass bulb containing mercury vapor at a low degree of pressure. An electrode is sealed into each end of the tubular bulb. When you impress the proper voltage on these electrodes, a flow of negatively charged electrons is attracted from one electrode to the other and the tube becomes luminous, the intensity of light being greatest near the center of the tube. The principal difference between lamp types is the means used to start the flow of electrons. With most lamps special starters are used, and the right voltage is impressed on the electrodes through ballasts, which are the small transformers that limit the electric current to the voltage needed by the specific tube. A fluorescent lamp includes more than just the tubular bulb which becomes luminous. One needs to think of it as a whole: the tube, the starters, and the ballasts.

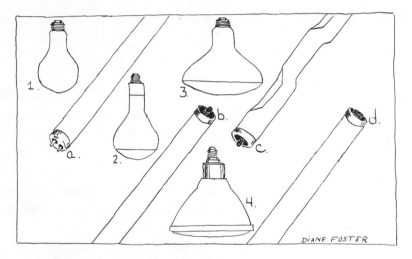

Lamps used in indoor gardening. Incandescent: 1. Standard bulb, 2. PS bulb, 3. R bulb, 4. PAR bulb; Fluorescent: a. 40-watt, b. T-10, c. Power-Groove, d. High Output.

Starters and ballasts for early lamps were bulky and complicated pieces of equipment, but modern ballasts are smaller and more reliable, and the number of auxiliary parts has been considerably reduced. Improvements have also been made in the starters. Lamps with separate switch starters have been used since the introduction of fluorescent lamps in 1938. This method made possible the use of smaller ballasts. There was always, however, a short interval of time before the lamps lighted after they were turned on. There is now available a rapid-start lamp which eliminates this and emits nearly 50 per cent more light than the older preheat tubes. This lamp is easily identified, for it has two pin contacts at each end of the tube, where the earlier lamps have only a single pin head.

Other changes and improvements in the fluorescent lamp have been made since we began gardening under lights in the 1940s. At that time there were only four lamp sizes; today dozens of standard sizes are available, and lamps range from six to ninety-six inches in length consuming from 4 to 215 watts. Fluorescent lamps are classified according to the amount of lamp currents they carry, as expressed in milliamperes, or MA. There are three general categories—light-, medium-, and heavy-load lamps—a recently established grouping that serves to eliminate the confusion caused by the many brand names used by the various manufacturers. Although you can get some results with only two light-load 40-watt tubes, most of the lamps used in horticulture are in the heavy-load category, with a range of 100 to 1500 MA. The table will give you a rough idea of the types of lamps available. We suggest that you buy lamps by the numbers of milliamperes rather than by the special trade names (such as VHO, meaning Very High Output, or SHO, Super High Output). With the exception of Power-Groove lamps, which are produced only by General Electric, the fluorescent lamps we are discussing are made by all major electrical companies.

In addition to the differences in operation, size, and light intensity, fluorescent lamps are also distinguished by the quality of their light, as it is measured in a color-temperature scale. You may have noticed that a standard coolwhite tube is given a color rating of 4500 degrees K. The K stands for Kelvin and indicates a temperature scale, just as in other temperature scales F stands for Fahrenheit and C for Centigrade. For example, water boils at 212 degrees Fahrenheit, at 100 degrees Centigrade, and at 373 degrees Kelvin.

Color temperatures refer to the color produced during the heating of a metallic object. Practically everyone has heated a piece of metal over a flame at some time, and has noticed that as the metal becomes hot it starts to glow with a color that changes from a deep red to orange, and if the metal is allowed to become hot enough, it becomes almost white in color. It is possible to determine an apparent color temperature of a hot object by measuring the amount of light it emits at different colors. This color temperature is a measure of the relative amounts of the various colors in the light and does not refer to the total intensity or brightness of the light. A small fluorescent desk lamp, for example, will have a higher color temperature but a lower brightness than a large incandescent street lamp.

The coolwhite fluorescent tube is the traditional lamp of the indoor gardener, although recent studies have shown that the warmwhite fluorescent tube is equally effective. The name is printed in small letters at the end of the tube. Be sure to notice this color-temperature rating when you buy lamps, since other types, such as "white" or "daylight" are not adapted for plant growth.

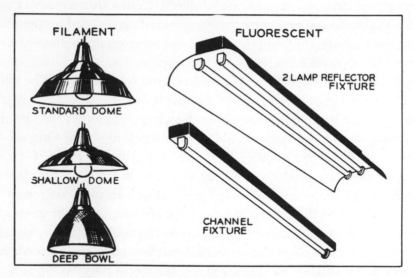

Types of reflectors useful for indoor gardening.
(*Courtesy General Electric*)

When selecting your lamps, you must also give thought to the fixtures. Fixtures come in many sizes and lengths, although they are standardized so that different tubes of the same length may be interchanged. You can obtain fixtures with reflectors that hold one, two, three, or four tubes. Be sure to buy porcelain-coated reflectors, as they are far more effective than those coated with baked enamel and are worth the slightly higher price. Narrow, boxlike fixtures to hold a single tube are made without reflectors and are sold as channel fixtures or strips. This compact form makes them of great value to lamplight gardeners because they can be mounted close together, giving out more light in a small space than you can get any other way. Channel-type fixtures must be specially mounted and wired, but their cost is low as compared with the reflector type. If you decide to use these channel fixtures with 1500 MA tubes the proportion of incandescent light must be raised to as much as 40 watts for every 100 watts of fluorescent light. Most fixtures come equipped with rubber-coated cords that need only be plugged into an outlet.

Fluorescent tubes do not need to be mounted in fixtures. You can simply mount sockets on a metal board and slip the tubes into them. Although we used masonite instead of metal boards in our early work, we were using low-intensity lamps that did not create a fire hazard. The lamps manufactured today, however, are of a much higher intensity and we must caution you against the use of any flammable material near the tubes. A custom-made installation is very useful if you are constructing your own planter or decorative case, but you will need the services of an experienced electrician, as the ballasts and wires must be specially installed. Booklets containing directions for installing your own ballasts are available from several of the major electric companies (see Appendix IV).

❁ *The Incandescent Lamp*

The incandescent lamp is so familiar that it scarcely needs a description. In a filament bulb the current flows from one lead wire to another through the solid tungsten wire. This heats the wire to incandescence and produces light.

The temperature at which it operates is higher than any other artificial heat ordinarily encountered by man—a temperature at which asbestos or fire brick would melt like wax in a furnace, and twice the temperature of molten steel. Although the filament is heated to give a temperature of 5000 degrees Fahrenheit, it does not burn up because it is either in a vacuum or surrounded by inert gases that do not combine chemically with the tungsten. These facts explain why tungsten-filament bulbs generate more heat than fluorescent tubes.

New lamps with built-in reflectors help in offsetting the effects of the heat. They resemble the standard incandescent lamp, but have a dark appearance over much of the bulb because of the sealed-in reflector. This reflector is useful in several ways. Because it is built in it stays brighter longer, cannot accumulate dirt, and never needs cleaning. Far more important, however, is the fact that it serves to conduct the heat upward instead of permitting it to shine downward on the plant-growing area. Some manufacturers claim that the downward flow of the heat is reduced by as much as 70 per cent. Accordingly the incandescent lamps with built-in reflectors are often referred to as cool-beam. The General Electric Company, following the modern trend of referring to everything by initials, calls the lamp made for indoor use the R bulb, or the Reflector bulb. Other companies usually use its full name. The R bulb is made in 30 to 1000 watts. The small size is very effective as it gives off so little heat, and several of them can be used in place of one large bulb. The reflector lamp made with molded glass especially for outdoor use is known as PAR, or Parabolic Aluminized Reflector. The plain reflector lamp can be used out of doors too, but it needs to be well protected, for it breaks on exposure to moisture while the PAR does not.

The simplest way of controlling the amount of heat generated by unfiltered incandescent bulbs is to use several bulbs of low wattage instead of one or two large bulbs. In this way the heat is distributed over a larger area. A more effective and strongly recommended device is the use of a shield. A shield can be made with a sheet of glass, plexiglass, or clear plastic mounted in a frame an inch or two below the lamps. The shield keeps the heat away from the plants and, although there is a slight loss in light intensity, the lower temperature greatly improves the quality of the growing conditions.

Perhaps the most spectacular recent development in indoor gardening is the revival of the incandescent lamp. Because it gives off so much heat, many gardeners had banished the incandescent lamp and turned to lamps whose color enhanced plant appearance without producing as satisfactory growing conditions.

But careful research on the part of plant physiologists has reversed the role of the incandescent bulb. Fluorescent and incandescent lamps differ greatly in the proportions of red and far-red rays produced in their white light. Sunlight, although much more intense, contains about the same relative proportion of red and far-red energy as does the incandescent light. Light from fluorescent lamps, on the other hand, is high in both blue and red rays, but is extremely low in the important far-red. It is the far-red that makes for flowering, for germination of light-sensitive seeds, and for many other plant responses. The importance of reintroducing incandescent lighting in home-gardening installations was immediately recognized. Research scientists began investigating the effect of far-red light, and indoor gardeners developed effective ways of circumventing the heat it generated.

✿ *Special Plant-Growth Lamps*

When the reputation of the incandescent bulb was at its low ebb, special fluorescent phosphor lamps were developed to use in the home for growing plants. These are sold commercially as Gro-Lux, Plant-Light and Plant-Gro tubes. As soon as the importance of far-red light in the growth of plants was understood, the Sylvania Company developed a Wide-Spectrum Gro-Lux unit to be used in a one-to-one ratio with the Gro-Lux tube. It is possible to achieve the same effect by using an incandescent bulb with Gro-Lux in a one-to-three ratio.

Plant physiologists and research directors do not generally favor these special lamps which are not used for research in any of the large laboratories or phytotrons. However, many amateurs are enthusiastic about them and feel that their orchids, African violets, and gesneriads grow better under these lamps than under any other. They like the fact that they do not need to use an incandescent bulb and they also like the way their plants look under these lights.

In order to increase the red and blue rays, manufacturers of the phosphor lamps reduce the output of the yellow-green rays, which affects the color of the light thrown onto the plants. Gro-Lux and Plant-Light tubes tend to cast a purplish light, while the Plant-Gro tube sheds a somewhat yellowish cast. Many people feel that the plants actually do look better under these lights, because green leaves appear darker green, nearly black. Other colors are enhanced; red seems redder, and so forth. This is only a visual effect, of course, since the plants become quite ordinary looking when placed under sunlight or the balanced artificial lighting produced by coolwhite tubes and incandescent bulbs.

Many decorators and homemakers have found that the special glow given by these special plant-growth lamps plays a definite part in their decorative schemes. One decorator we know used this effect to great advantage in an apartment where the dominant colors were purple, red, and yellow. Some of the plants were grown under a yellow Tiffany-glass shade with a Plant-Gro fluorescent tube made by Westinghouse. The yellow glow made an interesting contrast with the purple effulgence of Sylvania's Gro-Lux lamp, which the decorator used in other parts of the room.

In spite of these attractive qualities, however, we still prefer to grow and display plants that are *naturally* brighter and healthier when grown in the better conditions provided by balanced lighting. When we experimented with two identical cases, one using coolwhite fluorescent tubes and incandescent lamps and the other using Gro-Lux tubes, the plants grew much more luxuriantly in the first case than in the second. When incandescent lamps were added to the Gro-Lux tubes, however, the growth in that case increased perceptibly. The fact that we still preferred to see our plants displayed under a light as close to sunlight as possible, without the artificial glow, is purely a matter of personal taste.

❀ Lamps for Indoor Gardeners

A single fluorescent tube, an incandescent bulb, or even a table lamp can be an aid to the indoor gardener and will increase the growth of any plant placed beneath it. Of course, if you have a small lamp, the plant must also have some daylight. The lamps listed below are particularly recommended for those who wish to provide a special place for plants either in planters or in an indoor greenhouse. Remember that incandescent and fluorescent lamps should be used together in the same installation in the ratio of one to three. In practical terms this means that you should use 35 watts of incandescent for every 100 watts of fluorescent light. There are two more things to remember about these lamps. First, keep them clean. Dust seems to be inescapable, and dust on the lamps cuts down on their efficiency. Second, it is equally important not to let the fluorescent or incandescent lamps become darkened, as they do with use. Do not press them to their full life span. Plan on using them in indoor gardening for about 70 per cent of their estimated life.

Fluorescent Lamps

40-watt Tube (light-load)	This is the smallest lamp that can be used effectively in an installation. We recommend the use of at least two tubes, placed close to the plants. Estimated life: 12,000 hours.
Plant-Growth (medium-load)	These are the specially developed lamps which are recommended for amateurs who are willing to accept something less than truly balanced lighting. For best results, supplement them with incandescent bulbs or the special lamps developed to produce the far-red rays, such as Sylvania's Wide Spectrum. Estimated life: 7500 hours.
High-Output Fluorescent (medium-load)	We recommend the use of rapid-start rather than preheat tubes since they give nearly 50 per cent more light. Estimated life: 12,000 hours.
T-10 (heavy-load)	This lamp is especially designed for indoor gardeners and, combined with four, six, or eight similar tubes, will give the greatest possible light intensity in the smallest space. It has a built-in reflector. Our greatest success has resulted from the use of this tube with the reflector incandescent lamp in the ratio given above. Estimated life: 12,000 hours.

T-12 (heavy-load)	Also reflectorized, this lamp is designed for high-intensity lighting in research plant-growth chambers. Estimated life: 9000 hours.
Power-Groove	Made by General Electric, this tube is also designed for high-intensity growth chambers. It gives off approximately 25 watts per foot, the highest light output of any fluorescent lamp today. Its width, however, is a disadvantage, since eight T-10 lamps will fit into the space occupied by five Power-Groove lamps. Estimated life: 9000 hours.

Incandescent Lamps

Standard Tungsten Filament	If this bulb is used, a wide reflector that casts as much light downward as possible should be used with it. Estimated life: 750 to 1000 hours.
Reflector (R)	This is the recommended type of lamp for most installations because its reflector forces 70 per cent of the heat to be conducted upward, away from the growing area. Estimated life: 1000 hours.
Parabolic Aluminized Reflector (PAR)	This is weather resistant and is recommended for outdoor installations. Estimated life: 1000 hours.
PS	This pear-shaped reflectorized lamp needs protection from moisture. Estimated life: 1000 hours.

In all of our most successful cases we used a combination of T-10's coolwhite fluorescent and the Reflector incandescent lamps in a ratio of 40 watts of incandescent to 100 of fluorescent. As the sockets of both are interchangeable with those for other incandescent bulbs and fluorescent tubes, they can be used in any installation you plan. They produce plants growing beneath them that seem practically perfect.

 *4*

RESEARCH
THAT NEVER ENDS

In the science of growing plants in a controlled environment in the home, in schools, and in phytotrons, one experiment leads to another. It is a fascinating new field in which everyone can participate, and the opportunities for research are unlimited. Although electro-horticulture is a biological science, it is not limited to recognized scientists: the inexperienced novice and the devoted amateur can experiment with new light combinations and discover methods of value to their fellow hobbyists.

A young science student establishes a project on the dining-room windowsill. He is studying motion in plants, which is linked with varying light intensities, using the prayer plant and sorrel. How much artificial light does he need to add to keep them from folding their leaves at dusk? The whole family joins him in watching.*

A retired engineer experiments with specially wired fluorescent tubes and small heavy-duty incandescent bulbs to obtain a high enough light intensity to make miniature geraniums flower in his doll-house planter. Since flowering geraniums are often a disappointment to lamplight gardeners, it seems doubtful that the experiment will work. But it does work, and a gold certificate awarded to his project at

* See Appendix III for list of experiments.

the International Flower Show in New York City underlines his success.

Will man's ability to duplicate in small growth areas the light intensity of the sun at midday, 10,000 foot-candles, add new understanding to the fundamental process of photosynthesis? Dr. R. J. Downs, directing research at the North Carolina State University phytotron, has discovered new light combinations that have made further investigations possible.

The lights that Dr. Downs has used may become the indoor gardening lights of the future. Lucalox, metal-halide, and mercury lamps are as unknown to most of us as fluorescent and incandescent lamps are familiar. None of the three lamps alone produces good results in flowering or growing plants, but the lucalox lamp combined in the wattage ratio of one to one with either the mercury lamp or the metal-halide has proved very effective. The construction, operation, and radiation of the lucalox lamp is quite unlike that of the other high-intensity-discharge lamps.

Dr. Downs has described the kind of plant growth obtained with these lamps, but the simple details of their use is being made available to indoor gardeners for the first time in this book. He has been able to promote excellent plant growth in a wide variety of species: tobacco, cotton, cucumbers, peanuts, radishes, collards, and cockscomb, to name only a few.

Two sizes of lucalox lamps are available, one with a wattage of 275, the other with a wattage of 400. The mercury lamps come in many different watt sizes, but the metal-halide at present comes in only two sizes: 400 watts and 1000 watts. Metal-halide lamps are called Multi-Vapor lamps by General Electric and Metal-Arc by Sylvania.

Metal-halide lamps are used in many indoor shopping malls. A forward-looking decorator can add lucalox lamps of equal wattage to the installation and grow flowers that usually are associated only with outdoor gardens. These metal-halide lamps are used in many of the major stadiums because they give the kind of light needed for color telecasts without requiring huge increases of power.

A lucalox lamp of 275 watts combined with an equal wattage in mercury lamps will give the home gardener a summerlike spot in the living room where he can garden while the snow piles deep. The high light intensity will enable him to choose the flowers he particularly enjoys and they will grow as if they were in full sunshine.

The equipment needed to operate these lamps represents an initial investment of seventy-five to one hundred fifty dollars, but the estimated life of a mercury lamp is over 24,000 hours. Happily, according to Dr. Downs, the Wide-Lite Company in Houston, Texas, is developing a fixture especially designed for the homeowner to use with mercury and lucalox lamps.

If hearing of these brilliant illuminations should discourage you from growing flowers with the lamps you now have, you need only remember that the growth habits of plants work in your behalf. Through the ages plants have adjusted to the natural fluctuation of light that may reach their leaves. Clouds, rain, and shadows from other plants can greatly decrease the light available to them. Too, different species absorb different amounts of the light that fall upon their leaves, anywhere from 15 to 40 per cent. Yet in full sunlight only about 3 per cent of the light absorbed is used in photosynthesis. As the amount of light decreases, however, the amount of light-energy used for photosynthesis *increases tenfold*. This is an important biological fact that makes lamplight gardening in the home possible.

Increasing the light intensity that a hobbyist could obtain in the home was the aim of Francis C. Hall when he built a doll-house planter in which he grows miniature geraniums that flower to the same brilliant red as the simulated brick on the outside of the planter. It is a simple formula. His 30-watt coolwhite fluorescent tubes are equipped with rapid-start ballasts normally used in 40-watt tubes. This results in about 30 per cent more light because the tubes are operating not on 75 volts, but on 100–105 volts. This overballasting is a standard practice in photography and in some other fields where a high degree of light is needed from a small tube. It slightly shortens the life of a tube but in a small planter this is not a handicap.

The incandescent bulbs he uses are not of the standard type with which we are familiar in homes and offices. Standard bulbs are rated at 120 volts. The voltage is printed in small letters at the glass end of the bulb under the wattage figure. The bulb that Mr. Hall uses is 130 volts. It is extensively used in industry in inaccessible places because the heavier filament allows it to burn twice as long. These bulbs can be bought in any electrical supply store in the same wattage and at the same price as the standard bulbs.

Mr. Hall uses a series of twelve 15-watt bulbs in his doll house placed close together between the six specially wired 30-watt cool-white fluorescent lamps. The incandescent bulbs scarcely feel warm to the touch. Under these two types of lamps his miniature geraniums blossom beautifully, which is proof of sufficient light intensity. In our cases with 1500 foot-candles geraniums blossomed, but not with the gay abundance that they do in Mr. Hall's doll house.

5

MEASURING

LIGHT INTENSITY

Foot-candles are the standard unit for measuring light intensities, just as inches are a measure of length. Sometimes it is possible to guess how many inches long a table or a bench may be, but guessing light intensities is much more difficult. Our eyes are poor gauges, for they adjust so easily to different conditions that we can even "see in the dark."

A number of meters, some quite simple and others very complicated, are manufactured for measuring light. Probably the most familiar is the one used by photographers to determine the proper exposure for their films. Many of these meters—but not all—have scales in footcandles and can measure with reasonable accuracy the amount of light reaching your plants. There are inexpensive light meters available which are priced at about fifteen dollars and indicate light intensities of up to 1000 foot-candles.

Although a light meter is a pleasant luxury, and not actually essential in lamplight gardening, it is useful in that it has a tendency to prod you into devising ways to increase your light intensity, with a resulting improvement in your plants. Often you can borrow a photographic meter from a friend to check the amount of light reaching your plants. You will need to chart it only once for each arrangement, since, although both incandescent bulbs and fluorescent tubes emit less light as they grow older, the intensity does not change radically.

In any installation, there are two ways of increasing the light intensity: you can add more lights or you can grow your plants closer to the lights. Each year, during our experiments in working with lights, we changed the arrangement so that more lights could be added, and eventually practically doubled the light intensity.

The light intensity drops as the distance between plant and light increases, though the rate of decrease differs with fluorescent tubes and incandescent bulbs. For instance, if you prop a plant up so that it is twice as close to the filament bulb as when it is resting on the table, you will be giving it four times as much light. But if your table lamp happens to contain fluorescent tubes, you will only double the light reaching the plant by propping up the plant the same distance.

Regardless of what installation of lights you have, you will inevitably have some brightly illumined areas and others that are shaded. In lamplight gardening this is an advantage rather than a disadvantage, for some plants require more light than others. This makes it possible to grow shade-lovers and sun-worshipers together. In our tiny four-by-six-foot winter garden we have the lucerna begonia beneath the very center of the tubes so that the stately plant may have the fullest amount of light. In the shadow of its leaves some African violets are blossoming beautifully in a light intensity of 600 foot-candles, and practically hidden in the corner, under some spreading fronds of the fern, is the Christmas cactus, whose leaves curled up and wrinkled in the full light of the case.

In an effort to indicate the plants that can be grown under different types of lighting arrangements, three arbitrary classifications have been made. (See Appendix I.) In the first group are those plants which will grow in a light intensity of from 50 to 250 foot-candles; in the second, those that will grow well in a light intensity ranging from 250 to 650; in the third group are those that need a light intensity of from 650 to 1400 foot-candles. Of course, there is inevitably some over-lapping.

Most houseplants barely exist in a light intensity of 50 foot-candles; increasing it to 250 foot-candles transforms them into a luxuriant mass of foliage. In the second grouping, a light intensity between 250 and

650 foot-candles is the fairy godmother that makes ordinary house-plants—African violets, begonias, beleperone, and many others—blossom profusely; while the third category is the light intensity needed for starting seedlings for your garden and for growing the so-called "florist plants."

You can appreciate better how much light varies when you consider that at noon on a bright, sunny day the outside light intensity may be as high as 10,000 foot-candles, while on a cloudy day in winter it may be as low as 500 foot-candles. The light intensity is greater if you live in the mountains than if you live on the seashore, and if you live in western New York, where rain clouds sweep off the Great Lakes, you take low light intensities as a matter of course.

Indoor light intensities are much lower. One December we charted the amount of light reaching our plants in a windowbox in the dining room. Aside from one day when the light meter recorded 125 foot-candles, the daily average was between 22 and 35 foot-candles, Small wonder the plants in that window grew so slowly!

The accompanying chart gives the approximate foot-candle values of two 40-watt fluorescent lamps in a standard fixture, with a 12-inch reflector, when the plants are from six to eighteen inches below them.

Valuable as foot-candle meters are as a tool of measurement, they have one drawback: they measure only the light that the human eye sees, they do not measure far-red light. The discovery of phyto-chrome and the knowledge of its importance to plant growth heavily underlined the need for a portable meter that would accurately measure the three light rays (blue, 450; red, 650; and far-red, 730 nanometer units), the rays that make indoor gardening possible, and cause plants to grow.

The spectroradiometer was designed for this purpose. With this meter, it is possible to measure small segments of the light in both the visible and the near-visible spectrum reflected on plant leaves. One kind of spectroradiometer uses sixteen fixed wave-length settings from 370 to 1000 nanometers. The wave-length selector switch also adjusts the sensitivity for each channel so that measurements are read directly. Others operate on somewhat different principles.

Plant physiologists are very excited over the possibilities of these portable meters. They feel it will bring in a new era. Home gardeners

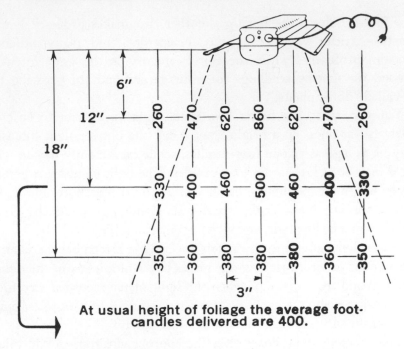

6"

12"

18"

260 — 470 — 620 — 860 — 620 — 470 — 260

330 — 400 — 460 — 500 — 460 — 400 — 330

350 — 360 — 380 — 380 — 380 — 360 — 350

3"

At usual height of foliage the average foot-candles delivered are 400.

Foot-candles delivered at various distances from lights.
(*Courtesy General Electric*)

may not immediately feel the need of one, but the meters offer many opportunities for special investigation by students in schools and colleges.

Indirectly, they will encourage more careful reading with the foot-candle meter. Instead of citing a reading of 1200 foot-candles as the light intensity in an indoor garden, one can read 1000 foot-candles of fluorescent light and 200 of incandescent, at a certain distance from the lights. This specific reading makes it possible to duplicate the same lighting elsewhere. The type of light given off by different fluorescent lamps varies greatly, and, of course, the light from an incandescent bulb has quite special qualities. (See Chapter 3.) In other words, the foot-candle meter measures only the degree of illuminance, while the spectroradiometer enables the scientist to determine the exact quality of the light present at any given time.

THE IMPORTANCE

OF TEMPERATURE

You can do much to counteract the effects of low light intensities by lowering the temperature. Although it is known that plants in the home respond better when the temperature is not above the middle seventies, this knowledge is rarely put into use. Most of us like our homes snug and warm in the wintertime, and though a number of houseplants might prefer a different atmosphere, they have had to live in the one we like.

We tested the effect of a living-room temperature on a group of our seedlings—both annuals and vegetables. We did not expect the results to be particularly outstanding in a temperature of almost 75 degrees Fahrenheit both day and night, but we were agreeably surprised. In a month's time everything was ready to be transplanted into the garden, after being kept out of doors for a few days.

Night temperatures are far more important than most of us realize. Plants gather their food during the day, but they digest it during the night hours, and the process is helped by a cool temperature. In fact, in horticultural circles, when temperatures are discussed, night temperatures are the ones referred to; day temperatures are not considered so vital. A knowledge of this may encourage you to turn down the thermostat at night, not only to save fuel but to help your plants toward better growth.

Ideally you should have lights installed in at least two locations, with different ranges of temperature. The lowest should be between 50 and 60 degrees; the other, between 60 and 70 degrees Fahrenheit at night.

If it is possible to hang your lights in two such spots, you can grow any houseplant and start enough vegetables and flowers to overrun a city lot. Commercial growers have both warm and cool greenhouses, and you will do well to follow suit.

It is not as difficult as it seems at first to find these varied ranges of temperature in our modern, uniformly heated homes. Our former coal bin stands out to us as an example. For years after we had stopped burning coal in our furnace it had been a general catch-all, but when we discovered that its temperature during the greater portion of the fall and winter was between 50 and 60 degrees Fahrenheit, there was a general housecleaning. Now it is a place of beauty, where cool-loving flowers bloom and golden balls of Boston lettuce furl their leaves. Unless you test such odd corners with a thermometer in hand, you may pass them by and thereby miss the fun of growing many plants that insist on cool pillows at night. You may, of course, have space for only one set of lights; in that case, the important thing is to have the temperature as low and as constant as possible. Where this is impractical, grow the plants that can survive the temperatures you have.

We had a number of African violets which bloomed gaily at 85 degrees Fahrenheit. Their blossoms were smaller and did not last as long as some grown in a steady environment of 68 degrees Fahrenheit, but they were beautiful to behold. Your flowers can be, too. With good care, they adjust to temperatures not quite to their liking. The lovers of warmth are as beautiful as those that like it cool, and just as numerous.

HOW LONG THE NIGHT?

"How long the night?" is not a poetical question, but one of profound importance to lamplight gardeners faced with the necessity of making their own suns rise and set. The practical answer is that with foliage plants it makes little difference. They grow well in cycles in which the day and night are equal, and just as well when they are uneven, with eighteen hours of light and six of darkness. But plants that flower need to be studied. Here, as elsewhere, generalities are dangerous. Most bulbs, for instance, are not very particular about their day. Tulips, daffodils, and hyacinths will flower in a cycle of ten hours of light and fourteen of darkness, or the reverse. Freesias, on the other hand, if they are to produce their delicate, fragrant bells, must have a lamplight day which lasts only ten hours, and fourteen hours of darkness.

Darkness is as vital to houseplants as light is. Not recognizing this, one of our friends, attracted by lamplight gardening, put his plants under lights and left them there. At first they grew so fast that he felt confident this was the proper treatment; but after three weeks of constant lamplight the leaves dropped off, the stems began to shrivel, and our friend's faith in growing plants by lamplight was shattered.

The longest day we have given our plants is eighteen hours; nine hours has been the shortest. Fastidious ones take special care. A small amount of additional light may do strange things.

The story is often told in horticultural circles of the florist whose chrysanthemum buds remained furled in tiny green balls when December snows were flying. His growing conditions were excellent, but the chrysanthemums did not open or show any response to his well-directed efforts.

"Why?" was the question always on his lips.

It was answered when he brought a friend into the greenhouse late one night. The bright lights of a moving-picture marquee across the street illumined the greenhouse so that it was as bright as in the daytime.

"That's the gremlin," said his friend, pointing to the lights. "Shade your chrysanthemums, and they will blossom." As soon as shades were installed to shut out the offending rays, the chrysanthemums burst into bloom.

Chrysanthemums are so sensitive that some firms now sell them tagged and labeled as to their light requirements. By meeting these demands, florists have found it possible to have "mums" the year around.

Too much light proved to be a similar problem in the case of the poinsettias a friend of ours was blithely growing. We admired her gardening skill, for only the very brave will try to grow poinsettias in their homes because of the numerous pitfalls that are always present. But she waved doubts aside. She had grown a number of healthy-looking slips from the parent plant. They had been kept out of doors all summer, and had survived the transfer indoors without losing a leaf. She was looking forward to a window full of glowing blossoms at Christmastime.

But her hopes fell as the time drew near and the beautiful colored bracts were not forthcoming. In this instance the gremlin was her own reading lamp. The poinsettia, too, needs a short day. The light from the lamp had lengthened it by three or four hours. When she discovered the trouble she began to place the plants, without fail, in a dark closet every evening at six, and to take them out the next morning at eight, or sometimes later. The treatment worked, and the poinsettias obligingly produced their display for Valentine's Day instead of Christmas.

Plants whose light requirements are very specific will need particular attention. They may be established in different growth areas where lights are turned on and off to suit their needs; or they may be treated like babies, taken away from the plant family and put to bed early; or, like adolescents, they may be allowed to stay up part of the night.

African violets, when given eighteen hours of lamplight and a light intensity of around 650 foot-candles, produce an abundance of flowers (see diagram).

LIGHT	600 FOOT-CANDLES		
TIME	6 HRS.	12 HRS.	18 HRS.
LEAVES	44.6	54.3	55.7
FLOWER STALKS	18.9	22.6	28.3
FLOWERS	92	180.8	239

(AVERAGE NUMBER PER PLANT)

Dramatic results in African violet culture obtained by increasing hours of light. (*Courtesy General Electric*)

This response of plants to differing periods of day and night is known as photoperiodism. The principle was discovered by two government scientists, W. W. Garner and H. A. Allard, who were working to determine why a certain variety of tobacco plant, Maryland Mammoth, failed to produce seed in the vicinity of Washington, D.C., when it was successfully grown somewhat farther south. They had carefully investigated many different factors known to affect blossoming and seed production, without finding any answer. Finally they mechanically shortened the length of the day for the plant by placing it in a completely dark enclosure every afternoon at four o'clock. Every plant whose day was so controlled produced seed in time for harvesting, while the others, left to nature's administration, failed to set seed.

The reaction of these tobacco plants uncovered this new principle. It proved that light intensity and temperature were not the deciding factors in production of flowers and seed in plants, but that successive *rhythmic* periods of darkness and light were.

In the light of this discovery, Garner and Allard worked out an entirely new method of plant classification. Plants which needed more hours of daylight than of night were called "long-day plants"; those that needed fewer hours of daylight than of night were called "short-day plants"; those that seemed indifferent to the length of day and night were known as "day-neutral."

It is important for lamplight gardeners to understand this method of classification, for it may make the difference between flowers and the lack of them. Happily, the great majority of houseplants can be treated as belonging to the day-neutral class. They will blossom in varying degrees of abundance, whether you give them a lamplight day of twelve, fourteen, sixteen, or eighteen hours.

But a short-day plant absolutely will not give forth a single blossom unless, while its buds are forming, it has ten hours of lamplight and fourteen hours of darkness.

Vegetables, as well as annual and perennial flowers, should have as long a day as possible, as each extra hour of light increases their growth. They will grow, however, whether they are given a fourteen-hour or an eighteen-hour day. As vegetables are foliage plants, when they are young no law of photoperiodism is involved.

Photoperiodism is a wide-open field for investigation. Plant scientists are experimenting with its many different phases, with something of the breathless excitement that geologists look at moon dust. They have discovered a principle that has never been known to man before, and the results are life-giving. But because it is such a new field there are many things that even an amateur can discover under his lights. We felt we were in a new world when, under lights, our cyclamen became ever-flowering.

Unless you are a born night owl, it is difficult to give your plants an eighteen-hour day. There are two alternatives. You can sacrifice some additional illumination (and some blossoms) and turn your lights on and off to suit your own waking and sleeping habits; or you can install a timer. Electric-supply houses sell many types of timers; or a poultry timer, such as farmers have long found useful in getting their chickens up, may be ordered from a mail-order house. Any timer can be adjusted so that it will automatically give your plants an eighteen-hour day and a six-hour night.

Of course this is practical only when the plants you have grouped together under the lights in your greenhouse or over a bench require the same length of day. A timer could, of course, be adapted to a single lamp, but it hardly seems worth the trouble. If you are using individual lamps, it is generally necessary to turn them on and off by hand. The danger in this method is that too often one forgets the importance of the word "rhythmic." Plants thrive on regularity rather than on days that vary from six to twelve hours in length. Occasional forgetfulness can be forgiven, but it should not become chronic.

Perhaps one of the secondary reasons for building an indoor greenhouse is that you can install a timer which will keep your "suns" rising and setting, so that you can forget them as completely as you forget Old Sol.

✿ ✳ ❧ ✺ ❀ ✳ *8*

THE ROLE
OF CARBON DIOXIDE

Bread from heaven comes in strange ways as scientists press their research in growing plants under the controlled conditions that gardening under lights makes possible. One breakthrough follows another, and one of the most exciting is being able to enrich the environment in which plants grow by adding more carbon dioxide in the daytime than is normally found in the atmosphere. Researchers have been able to make the petunia flower in five weeks from the time the seed was sown by adding from three to five times as much carbon dioxide to its environment as it normally expects. Experiments carried out in The Netherlands, in the United Kingdom, in Germany, and in the phytotrons and growth-control rooms in the United States show that the yields of lettuce, tomatoes, cucumbers, radishes, and many flowers (ageratum, snapdragon, and chrysanthemum) are doubled through the use of atmospheres enriched with carbon dioxide.

We had read of some of these results, but it had never occurred to us to apply it in any of our small growth-control rooms. The stimulus came as an unexpected and unsought dividend from helping some science students and a teacher whom we knew work out some meaningful experiments in a botany class.

Gardening under lights has opened new worlds for students of botany both in high schools and in colleges. It has given to botany the pragmatic approach, and is lifting it from a study where there is nothing to do to one that students find so interesting that they work on projects at home as well as in school. Life-science students can make real progress in a growth-control setup that includes only a few incandescent lamps and fluorescent tubes, or they can enjoy the elaborate facilities that many universities have to offer.

The class in which we were interested was studying photosynthesis, the process in which carbon dioxide is taken from the air and oxygen returned to it, the process by which a plant grows. One of the students, whose father worked in an ice-cream company where dry ice was readily available, suggested that he bring some to school to try the effect of carbon dioxide in their growth-control greenhouse. The students put the dry ice in a small dish and placed it in a box in the greenhouse. A perforated tube was fitted into the box and was carried through the small greenhouse. The greenhouse was closed and its vents stopped. The dry ice evaporated, giving off carbon dioxide. The students had no way of measuring the amount of carbon dioxide that was given off, but by their computations they figured it was between 4½ and 5½ per cent. We did not check their computations, but we were more tongue-tied than the students when we saw the effect on the plants. The leaves doubled in size, some small dwarf marigolds that had been grown from seed immediately flowered. Every plant became bushier. To the poetic, it seemed as though Queen Mab had waved a wand; to the practical, it seemed that this was indeed a way to grow food fast. You could almost see the plants grow. Certainly to every student it was a dramatic illustration of photosynthesis. We could scarcely wait to get some dry ice and see what would happen to our plants. It had a stupendous effect on both the growth of seedlings and the multiplying of flowers.

We placed the dry ice in a chute that was connected to a window at one end and to the greenhouse at the other. We stopped off all the ways in which the air could escape, closed the window, and plugged in the small fan in the chute, which blew the carbon dioxide into the greenhouse. Our light intensity was about 1500 foot-candles; the humidity was pretty constant at 57 per cent; and the temperature was high, between 80 and 85 degrees Fahrenheit. Although we used the dry ice only two or three times a week, our plants responded quickly. The radishes that we happened to have tucked in a pot in one corner were ready for eating in just a few days.

Dry ice is not the accepted way of bringing carbon dioxide into greenhouses, but it is a simple means if you have a source available. Safe and economical units which burn either natural or propane gas, with no unconsumed fumes, are not difficult to obtain. One can also buy carbon dioxide in a small cylinder and release it through a valve into the greenhouse. This is a simple means of getting the gas, if one is in the habit of handling chemicals. We never quite got around to trying it, because we moved to another house just as the experiment was about to begin. But it should not be difficult for an amateur to do.

Mr. S. H. Wittwer of the Michigan Agriculture Experiment Station, one of the pioneers in this country in studying the effect of increased carbon dioxide in plant atmospheres, says that carbon dioxide has given the most spectacular yield increase of any growth factor yet discovered in the culture of greenhouse crops. He likens the accomplishments with carbon dioxide to those which occurred a century ago when the benefits of chemical fertilizer were first used in crop production. With such an endorsement, indoor greenhouse enthusiasts should certainly try using this new substance, whether the carbon dioxide comes from a cylinder, a burner, or from evaporating dry ice. Caution must be exercised with the use of carbon dioxide. You should install a meter in the greenhouse to measure the percentage of concentration in the atmosphere. The carbon dioxide should not exceed 5 per cent, since too much of it can do considerable damage. But one need only look at the photograph of the petunia (see illustrations following p. 148) which blossomed in six weeks with a carbon-dioxide-enriched atmosphere, to fully appreciate its value.

LESSONS FROM

PHYTOTRONS

The phytotron is the crowning achievement made possible by the discovery that plants can be grown indoors under lights without the aid of natural light. These scientific laboratories are such a new development that to many the name itself is unfamiliar. Yet they have been built not only in the United States, but in Australia, Belgium, France, The Netherlands, Sweden, and Russia. In these buildings plants are grown under controlled conditions of light, temperature, and relative humidity, and attention is given to the many other factors that affect plant growth.

Although these chambers have many scientific features that one might not wish to incorporate into a growth-control room in a home or a school, a study of the highest in engineering achievement is certain to be of value to gardeners under lights everywhere.

Some of the controls used in these rooms would be very expensive for an individual to include in an already established growth room. But simple means of obtaining excellent growth of houseplants can be found in Chapter 11.

To give you a more graphic idea of what phytotrons actually are, we will describe the one at North Carolina State University in Raleigh. It is a four-story building with some fifty or more individually controlled areas for growing plants: various-sized growth-control chambers lighted with artificial lamps, several unlighted rooms, some seed germination cabinets, and also some glass greenhouses.

There are three sizes of plant-growth-control chambers. The larger ones are 8 feet by 12 feet by 7 feet from floor to light barrier; and 4 feet by 8 feet by 7 feet from floor to light barrier. The smallest is 3 feet by 4 feet by 4 feet from floor to light barrier.

In each of the chambers, the lights are separated from the plant-growing area by a piece of plexiglass. In one of the large walk-in rooms (shown in a photograph following p. 148), there are eighty-four 8-foot coolwhite fluorescent lamps equipped with reflectors, and forty-eight 100-watt incandescent bulbs used to increase the red and far-red radiation. The fluorescent lamps are 96 inches long and are known as T-12 1500 milliampere (abbreviated MA) lamps. Lamps in the smaller chamber are the same type, but are only 48 inches long. There are, in addition to these, incandescent filament lamps in the ratio of 1 to 3 by wattage. The temperature in these rooms can be set anywhere between 20 and 120 degrees Fahrenheit. Air at constant temperature is circulated in the rooms. The light intensity in the larger chambers can be maintained at 500 foot-candles, half that of sunlight on very bright days. In the smaller chambers, the light intensity is 300 foot-candles.

All of these plant-growth chambers are built of Alcoa aluminum panels, which consist of two layers of aluminum with a two-inch layer of polyurethane insulation between them. The inner surfaces have an Alzak finish, which is highly reflective. In the walls are a number of small fans to circulate air, electric heaters, and also cooling coils. The air leaves the chambers through grilles near the floor, passes through air ducts in the walls over the heaters or cooling coils, and then re-enters the chambers at the top just below the light barrier. Coming in from above, the air first strikes the tops of the plants. The downward flow aids in maintaining uniform temperature throughout.

Indoor temperature is about the only environmental variable that can be controlled and measured accurately for a reasonable cost, phytotron experts point out. Yet it ranks second to light in affecting plant growth. One has only to consider the effects of climate to appreciate this. The warm climate of the southland produces palms; the cold sweeps of the north, scrub pines.

Home gardeners can be encouraged by the fact that the temperature throughout the North Carolina State University phytotron is held at 75 degrees Fahrenheit, the temperature of many homes. It is raised or lowered in the individual growth rooms according to the demands of the experiment. To illustrate how important they regard the effect of temperature on plant growth, round chart-recording thermometers have recently been installed on each controlled-environment unit. If there is any malfunctioning in the temperature control in any of the experimental laboratories, it is immediately recorded. A distant control-checking system was not considered accurate enough. So, watch your thermometer! It can mean much to the plants you are growing.

Most homes today have thermostatic controls that allow you to investigate for yourself which plants will grow well in the temperature in which you live. Decorators can select the right plants for public buildings by checking the temperature controls, and you can establish in your own indoor greenhouse thermostatic controls which make true scientific investigation possible, even in a very small space.

Relative humidity, even in the phytotron, is only approximate, but is adjustable over a wide range from 60 to 95 per cent. They gain high humidities by spraying deionized water into the airstream in each chamber. Only a few chambers are capable of maintaining less than 60 per cent relative humidity, which is dry for most plant growth.

In small installations a relative humidity of between 60 and 65 per cent can be maintained almost without effort by putting flat galvanized pans filled with water in the bottom of the chamber, with hardware screen covering the pans for the flowerpots to stand on. Instruments that measure the relative humidity in small greenhouses are easily obtained.

In the phytotron, ample provision is made for adjusting the photoperiod, or the length of the day, because of its effect on so many species. The lights in the chamber are turned on by time switches, which are set so that each type of light can be turned on independently; thus the fluorescent lamps and the incandescent can be used together or separately depending on what is desired in an experiment.

These are what might be called the large-scale phytotron controls, but there are innumerable others. Increased attention is now being given to the many things that pollute the atmosphere. Automatic analyzers are being installed to measure low concentrations of ozone sulfur dioxide, and oxides of nitrogen and the aldehydes. Automatic systems to measure instantaneous changes in growth rate have been developed. The conductivity of the nutrient solution and concentrations of carbon dioxide in the atmosphere are controlled, and the reaction of the plant to all of these imposed conditions is carefully noted.

Because the science of growing plants under lights with a biological approach is such a new field, it offers opportunities to students in colleges and universities of varied service to mankind—from learning how to discover what are the right plants to adapt to hillsides denuded by forest fires, to discovering new cultivators and seeds that will bear fruit in various climates.

PART II

The Practical Application

10

GARDEN SITES

The development of high-intensity lamps in tubular, round, and square shapes has made it possible to grow plants and flowers nearly everywhere in the house, from the basement to the attic. Every lamp is a potential garden site, but before you launch your project it is a good idea to survey the field with your particular interests in mind.

Chinese cabbage, for instance, encased in an attractive jardinière under a living-room lamp, makes quite as interesting a bit of green as does sansevieria. It is nearly as hardy, and has the advantage that, in a hungry moment, you can chop it up and eat it. Most vegetables, however, do not lend themselves as gracefully to living-room culture. If you are a gardener interested in choice bits for the palate, you will do better to plan your garden in an out-of-the-way place. We did very well in a kitchen cupboard where we had two 40-watt fluorescent lamps. (Vegetables are foliage plants so they do not need an incandescent bulb.) Close to the kitchen sink the vegetables were easy to water and they grew so well that we had fresh salads the winter through. (See Chapter 26.)

A friend of ours moved into an apartment where the kitchen was lighted by unshaded warmwhite fluorescent tubes. She put some philodendron plants in large pots equipped with wick-watering (see p.

106) on the top shelf of a cupboard near the lamps. She then suspended a white trellis about four inches below the lights and trained the philodendron tendrils around it. The plants became the talked-about point in her kitchen. We were able to make a rather scraggly rubber plant interesting. We mounted three PAR incandescent bulbs in antique glass shades near the living-room ceiling. The rubber plant was placed in a large pot in a jardiniere with sphagnum moss packed around it. It was well watered and fertilized. The plant reached up for the light and grew practically three feet in a year's time. It also sent out two side shoots. Not surprisingly, the plant achieved more than stature: it became a focal point, both decoratively and conversationally.

Growing plants in kitchen cabinets.

Still, it must be admitted that fluorescent tubes and incandescent bulbs, the stock-in-trade of the lamplight gardener, are not exactly decorative accessories. The process of camouflaging them is often difficult. Bedrooms, back halls, and even closets can be good sites. We found a low-ceilinged closet off one of our halls especially useful. It was necessary only to add a small fluorescent fixture to the light that was already there in order to have excellent growing conditions. In two or three months this impromptu setting became so lovely that we wanted to share it.

If you are naturally meticulous about closets, showing them to guests presents no problem. But if you have the habit of thoughtlessly sticking an old umbrella or a slightly worn blouse in an out-of-the-way corner, the effect created by the flowers can be spoiled.

We finally decided to grow plants that made charming combinations in the open, and reserve the more remote spots for starting our vegetables, flowers, and cuttings for the garden. The best choice for these is a spot that is cool and fairly well ventilated. All vegetables, annuals, cuttings, and perennials grow somewhat stockier, and can be started earlier, if you can find a location where the temperature is somewhere between 55 and 65 degrees Fahrenheit. In our steam-heated homes it is often difficult to find such a place. It was this same difficulty that impelled one of our friends to install lights in his garage, where, from March to May, he grew enough plants to stock his own garden and those of his friends. Possibly the basement or attic will prove the ideal answer. These places may come to seem the most lived-in portions of your house, but, after all, by a very small investment you have increased your living space as well as added to the joys of living a hundredfold.

On the other hand, you may decide that the decorative advantages provided by your plants quite outweigh the disadvantages of the appearance of the lighting fixtures. You may discover that more sensational results can be achieved through combining a group of plants under lights than by buying a new piece of furniture. Take the hall, for example. Nothing will give a nicer welcome to your guests, or cause more exclamations, than ushering them into a garden spot where ferns and begonias have triumphed over coat hangers. Such a transformation is not difficult to accomplish. At most, it will involve installing a few lights and placing the plants beneath them.

We were especially successful with one of our halls, whose only claim to fame was an eighteenth-century card table with cabriole legs. Great-grandmother's table was quite forgotten, however, the moment we built a tiny glassed-in case, and filled it with flowers. We chose the far corner of the hall because of a homely little window there which added nothing to the décor but provided the ventilation to make the garden possible. This garden was lighted by two 40-inch-long Power-Groove fluorescent lamps and four incandescent lamps shielded by glass. There we grew bougainvillaea, flowering maple, African violets, and the ruffled cyclamen. We could scarcely get people out of the hall.

With lights and plants it is possible to transform even the furniture. One decorator proved this in a most original manner. Taking an old-fashioned golden oak table, she painted it, and had a round hole cut in the center, the same size as the overhanging fixture. A galvanized pan was sunk into this opening, flush with the tabletop. Plants were arranged in this and the pots concealed with peat moss, so that throughout the winter there was a garden on the table. Visitors who might have thought the table out of style found much to admire. In fact, it was so generally admired that a furniture designer actually made tables to be used in this way.

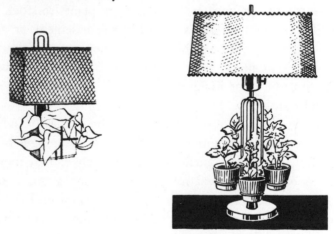

Lamp flower stands using incandescent light.

Numerous types of lamps are made today with dishes for holding plants as part of the design. In using them it is important to keep the lamps turned on during the day as well as in the evening.

The use of plants as an important aspect of decoration is finding advocates both in the home and in public and office buildings. There are innumerable possibilities. Plants can be grown on ledges a foot or two below fluorescent lamps installed in ceilings and in niches. Decorators have used plants as room dividers, with the aid of half-hidden lamps set into wooden frames. Willowy silk oaks (*Grevillea robusta*) and holly trees, placed in an entrance hall, can make an effective transition from the outside to the indoors. Hanging sedums can be used to reflect the graceful pendants of a crystal chandelier, and flowering plants of all kinds can be used as accents to any color scheme.

Lamps can also be combined effectively with groupings of plants in easily constructed planters, which you can make round or square, short or long, and finish to your taste to fit into your décor. One very popular design is illustrated. The drawing is not intended as a complete working diagram, but it will provide enough information for a skilled amateur or professional carpenter.

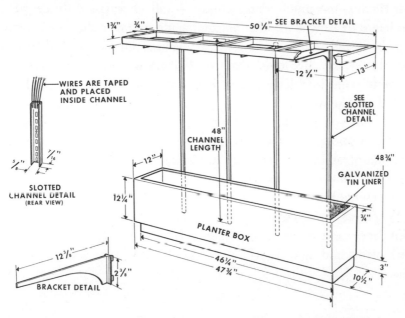

Construction plans for indoor garden for corridor or foyer, designed by Henry M. Cathey. (*Courtesy U.S. Department of Agriculture*)

Basically, a planter is just a wooden box or tub, protected on the inside either by stapling in two thicknesses of polyethylene or by a metal liner coated with asphalt so the zinc will not poison your plants. A planter will be more attractive, as well as more utilitarian, if you make a base for it that can be equipped with casters. Casters were popular with the Victorians, and though they fell into disrepute for a while, they are back in style again, along with Victorian furniture. So-called carpet casters, which are readily available, make it possible to move a heavy planter around the room, even over wall-to-wall carpeting.

Match the size of your planter both to the space you have available and to the type of lamps you want to use. Slotted metal channels fixed to the wall, such as those used for bookshelves, are used to support the lamp fixtures. The channels are strong, unobtrusive, and easily available in hardware stores. They make a fine place for taping and wiring the asbestos wires that lead to the fixtures and they can also support a shield of glass or plexiglass a few inches below the lamps. (If you find that there is too much glare, simply install fiberglass diffusers behind the lamps or have a wooden valance made to cover the fixtures.) You can also install a timer and mount the ballasts out of sight on the top of the planter. Be sure to mount the ballasts on pieces of metal; they generate considerable heat and it is not a good idea to attach them directly to the wood.

You can bolt panel fixtures for the fluorescent tubes to heavy angle irons attached to the channel supports or you can construct wooden mounting frames for them (see diagram). These frames are slotted on three sides and the tubes are slipped into the slots. The sockets for the incandescent bulbs are mounted on the fourth side of each frame.

Whatever arrangement you use, you will be sure to have flowers in abundance and many compliments from your friends. Decorating with plants and lights is still a new field and is very rewarding to explore.

Trough of well-arranged ornamental plants in a wall recess, lighted from above by one 40-watt white fluorescent lamp and two 75-watt R 30 incandescent lights. Designed by Dr. O. W. Davidson, Horticultural Department, Rutgers University. (*Photo courtesy Westinghouse*)

One end of a room becomes a conservatory with Tube Craft portable Flora-carts. (*Photo courtesy General Electric*)

French marigolds blossom under lights within four weeks' time after the seeds are planted. They are an excellent annual for growing under lights during the latter part of the winter and will continue to bloom until they meet their sisters in the garden. (*Photo by Frederick H. Kranz*)

Eight weeks from the day the seed germinates, tomatoes have flowers under lights. Save for the satisfaction of proving it can be done, it is wiser to transplant them to the garden earlier than this. (*Photo by Frederick H. Kranz*)

Sixteen Gro-Lux tubes give a rampant garden on a four-tier stand. (*Photo courtesy Sylvania Company*)

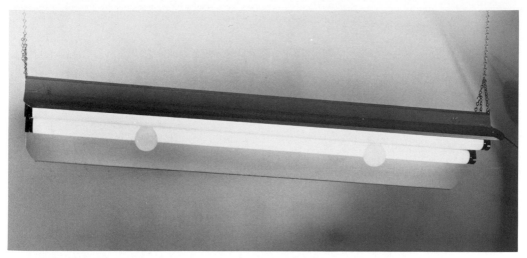

A fixture that combines incandescent and fluorescent light. (*Photo courtesy Floralite Company*)

Incandescent lights may be added to a Gro-Lux or fluorescent light growth area by putting the bulbs at the end of the fixtures.

The authors' 4-by-6-foot completely enclosed lamplight greenhouse. Such a structure must be built when there are bad fume conditions or if you need additional warmth. (*Photo by Frederick H. Kranz*)

Temperature plays an important part in the growth of flowers and vegetables under lights. Eighteen hours of lamplight and a temperature of 65 to 70 degrees —somewhat lower at night—is ideal for most plants. (*Photo by Frederick H. Kranz*)

Under artificial lights cuttings of evergreens, ornamental shrubs, and roses root quickly and with little difficulty. Photograph shows propagating box with glass-covered pots, and various rooted cuttings growing in the soil. (*Photo by Frederick H. Kranz*)

Chinese cabbage, Boston and New York State lettuce, radishes, onions, and endive can be grown under artificial lights so that you will have greens for your salad bowl throughout the winter. (*Photo by Frederick H. Kranz*)

An unused niche in the basement is transformed into a much-used area when the coming of spring presses every light into service for helping in the propagating of vegetables, shrubs, and garden annuals. (*Photo by Elizabeth L. Hahle*)

A GREENHOUSE

OF YOUR OWN

Where is the gardener who at some time or other has not wished for "a little greenhouse of his own"? Modern ways of life make it well-nigh impossible to have even a small glass structure, but by installing your incandescent and fluorescent lamps in a scientific ratio, you will have an excellent indoor equivalent. These tiny artificial illumined spaces have the advantage over the conventional structure, too, in being easier to construct and more economical to operate. They can be moved from place to place, so a change of location does not mean leaving your greenhouse behind. Best of all, during the dark, cloudy winters prevalent in many of our northern cities, plants receive more light and, consequently, grow better under these indoor conditions than they do in the small outdoor greenhouses of hobbyists. In fact, the United States Department of Agriculture's Yearbook predicts that the greenhouse under lights will be *the* greenhouse of the future. Handling "greenhouse" problems will prove a fascinating sport that will take you out of your armchair—and if you are not careful about the number of lights you install, keep you out of your bed.

A number of different installations are possible. You can buy stand-ard and custom-built commercial units for complete environmental control. You can also have the fun of assembling a unit with the exact tubes that you want at a considerable saving in price. The purchased units vary from large walk-in rooms to small reach-in cabinets, to carts supplied with tiers of lights that can be pushed from room to room. Some of these are shown in the sections of halftones following pp. 52 and 148.

A small greenhouse may be a pleasant addition to your living quarters. One of the most charming little greenhouses we have ever seen was the main feature in a dentist's waiting room. Completely finished to the smallest detail, this installation cost only thirty-five dollars to construct. According to the dentist, his patients were so interested in it that they lost their fears before his door. It was 2½ feet long, 18 inches deep, and 24 inches high, a size that could be adapted to many living rooms.

One group of students converted a cast-off refrigerator into a growth-control cabinet.* (Such a unit can often be bought for under thirty-five dollars, and makes an excellent dark-control cabinet, just as phytotrons have their dark chambers. It is essential in a variety of experiments, both with seeds as well as with plants that need complete darkness for a period.) This cabinet was used as both a dark and an illuminated one depending on the needs of the experiment. Coolwhite and warmwhite fluorescent tubes were used with incandescent bulbs, which meant putting in new thermostatic controls because the ones that came with the refrigerator were not suitable. But relatively little work was involved in the transformation, and it suggests a way that other students can construct a usable growth-control room.

All these structures pose a question of nomenclature. The uninitiated might take issue with calling any such installation a "greenhouse." One skeptic insisted they were merely terrariums, which have been used to grow flowers for years. But he ignored the important difference; these cases provide their own sunlight. Actually, as anyone who works with one of these tiny areas for growing plants soon discovers, it is an "indoor greenhouse" filled with flowers and greenery. You will be calling it that two weeks after your project is assembled.

You may want to begin by buying one of the small commercial

* Detailed instructions for doing this are given in the American Orchid Society's *Bulletin*, "Construction of an Inexpensive Growth Chamber for Orchids." *Bulletin 33: 102.* (See Appendices III and IV for other experiments and available pamphlets.)

arrangements that have been designed by several manufacturers and need only to be plugged into a convenient outlet. These small units have been made chiefly for growing African violets, although they can be used for other plants as well.

Shop around until you find a unit with a fixture that holds at least two, and preferably three, 40-watt coolwhite fluorescent tubes and that is wired also for incandescent bulbs. If the unit does not come equipped with 1500 MA lamps, you can put them in yourself since the tubes are interchangeable. And if the unit does not have incandescent lamps, it is possible to have them wired in. The difference it makes in the growth of your plants makes the effort of getting the right lamps in every unit well worthwhile. Your success with the ready-made units will surely inspire you to expand the project. It is far less expensive and much more rewarding to build a unit especially designed to suit your own needs.

Hanging your lamps in a reflector-type fixture over a bench is, of course, the simplest way of making a greenhouse. The fixture needs a firm support, so look for a joist in the ceiling. In some places, such as most basements, the joists are already exposed.

Unless you reflect the light that escapes at the sides back upon your plants on the bench, you will lose a lot of light energy. Our first makeshift arrangement was to hang sheets of white cloth around both the bench and the fixture, but we soon switched to masonite boards painted with white enamel. The masonite boards are placed along three sides of the lighted area, and will stand alone if holes are drilled in each piece of the board at the corners, and the sides tied in place with pieces of wire. A space of at least three inches is left open between the fixtures and the top of the board to provide ventilation.

When you buy your fixture, be sure that you have the electrical store attach an extension cord that will reach one of your wall outlets, so that you can plug it in just as you would a table lamp. Also at the electrical store, you can buy chain with which the fixture can be hung. Holes for this purpose have been punched through the metal at the ends of the fixture. The simplest chain to use for this purpose is one made of links that look like figure eights somewhat out of joint, for one of the loops is set at right angles to the other. The links of this chain can be opened by holding one end of a link in a vise, and prying open the other end with a pair of pliers. The sections of chain can then be separated. An opened link at one end of a length of chain can be used as a hook to fasten the chain onto the fixture.

A large screw-eye, nail, or hook may be used for fastening the chain from the fixture onto the joist. Before driving in the nail or the screw, drill a hole slightly smaller than the nail or screw into the floor joist.

The incandescent lamps that you need can also be hung from the joists. Purchase from a hardware store or electrical store extension cords of asbestos wire with lights attached in porcelain sockets, and add reflectors that cover the sides of the bulb, concentrating the light downward.

A workbench or an old table can be used for holding your plants, or you can use sawhorses and rest flats on them to hold your plants or a galvanized pan. Many people have had such fine results with an arrangement of this kind that they cannot see the value of a completely enclosed greenhouse, until they build one.

There are many advantages in having a completely enclosed greenhouse. You really have a growth-control chamber—your work will be more meaningful and your plants more beautiful. It ensures a higher humidity and also provides a means of circulating the air, which is essential to the health of the plants.

During the winter months the burning of fuel consumes such a large amount of air that the pressure inside the house is always appreciably lower than it is outdoors. Fresh air is constantly being sucked inside, so that ventilation problems are solved. But conditions are very different in the late fall and early spring, for the inward movement of the air is slight. It is then necessary to force fresh air to your plants from the out of doors.

We discovered this through hard experience. We could not understand why every spring so many of our plants stopped blooming and lost the glory of luxuriant foliage. We were convinced that our hot-water heater was emitting unconsumed gas fumes, and we went to all kinds of trouble and expense to get it corrected. Plants are particularly sensitive to these traces of unconsumed gas, which are so slight that humans are unaware of them, that they either cease to grow, do not blossom, or drop their leaves. There is a simple test to discover the presence of these fumes. Bring in some carnations. If their petals curl upward, partially consumed gas is present. Florists refer to this tendency of carnations to curl up their petals as "going to sleep." You may need to make more than one test, as carnations that are old will act in the same way.

But it was not the hot-water heater. That spring, in our completely enclosed case, the plants looked worse than before. It was some time before we had the answer—the ventilation was poor. We installed an electric fan and forced fresh air into the greenhouse and into the basement. The plants began to perk up. Within three weeks they had the healthy look we expected of plants grown under lights. It is often possible to ventilate an enclosed greenhouse with a natural draft. Holes may be made in the bottom of the greenhouse, and openings at the top. The movement of air from the bottom upward keeps it fresh.

There is, of course, no comparison in cost of operation between an indoor and an outdoor greenhouse. Indoors the only running expense is electricity. For many years the lights in our greenhouse used 12 kilowatts of electrical energy a day, which cost us eighteen cents. Even if your rates are somewhat higher, the cost will still be nominal.

CONSTRUCTING AN

INDOOR GREENHOUSE

Indoor greenhouses, even quite elaborate ones, are easy to make. The only tools you need are a crosscut saw, a square, a screwdriver, a hammer, and a pencil. A drill and a rabbet plane might help, but they are not essential. Anyone who is the least bit handy with tools can make one, and it will be a thing of beauty and a joy—perhaps not forever, but at least for many years.

You may have some old lumber about the house that can be pressed into service, but, if you must buy some, order Douglas fir, white fir, or yellow pine. Beware of spruce, as it inevitably warps badly. You will find the tubes and fixtures to be the most expensive items for your greenhouse. The wood, glass, masonite, and paint needed will not cost much. Even if you must have the services of a handyman the cost will be less than one-fifth of what you would have to pay to build an outdoor glass greenhouse of the same size.

We have built several indoor greenhouses—small, intimate ones, and large ones. Each winter we have three or more in use. Of the various types, our tall case, which is 42 inches high, 6 feet long, and 4 feet wide, is the easiest to construct. Too, its dimensions can easily be altered to suit any size of fixture. It can be built as an open case, or, with some additional work, completely enclosed. Invariably this is the one of our greenhouses that evokes the most admiration, possibly because it is tall enough so that the plants can be arranged in it to give the effect of a miniature garden.

We have illuminated this "garden" with various arrangements of light. Each change has given us a higher light intensity, pointing a moral for all indoor gardeners: study carefully your lights and how they are arranged. Higher light intensities inevitably mean more flowers. Plan your greenhouse so that you can use long tubes. Because the light intensity is lower at the ends of the tube, the longer the tube the greater the light intensity. The cases should be built a foot longer than the tubes. If you are using tubes 5 feet in length the case should be 6 feet; if you are using an 8-foot tube, the case should be about 9

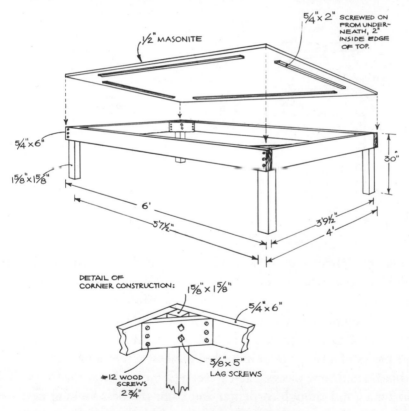

Design for an open plant bench.

feet long. This makes it much easier to mount the tubes, and gives you space at the ends where you can grow plants that do not need as high a light intensity.

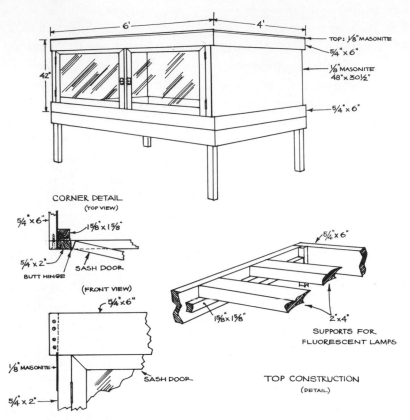

Design for simple indoor greenhouse.

The greenhouse itself is made separately from the supporting bench. To construct one 6 feet by 4 feet by 3½ feet, you will need four corner posts, each 42 inches long, cut from a clear two-by-four, ripped through the center. Most lumber yards will rip this for you when you buy it. The top and bottom of the frame are made from four pieces of 1¼-by-6-inch dressed lumber, 6 feet long, for the front and back, and four pieces, each 4 feet 2¼ inches long, for the ends. If you are a good enough carpenter and want the best-looking case possible, miter the ends to make a smooth corner. (In this case your end pieces will be only 4 feet long, instead of 4 feet 2¼ inches.) But do not try it unless you are really skilled, for it is difficult and a matter of appearance only. Structurally, the job will be as good if butt joints are made.

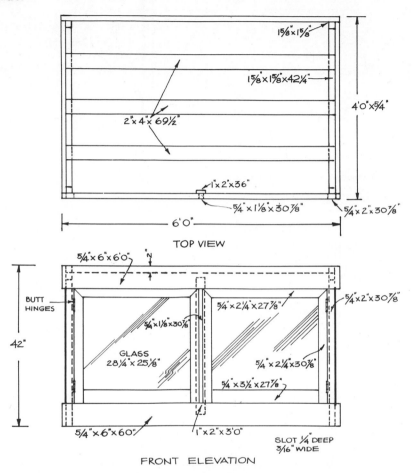

Plan and front elevation of indoor greenhouse.

With a rabbet plane, cut a slot about ¼ inch deep and ³⁄₁₆ inch wide along one edge of each of these pieces of wood, except for the two boards that are to be used on the front. These grooves are for the white-enameled masonite sides, which should be ⅛ inch thick. If no rabbet plane is available, two thin strips may be nailed on the edge of each board with brads, to form a slot. The sides and ends (both top and bottom) can then be fastened to the tops and bottoms of the posts

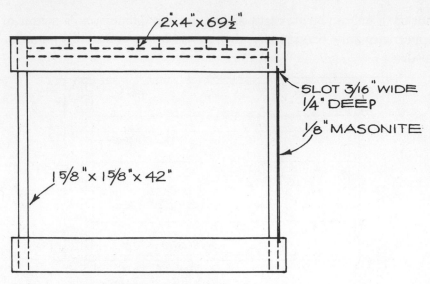

2"x4"x69½"

SLOT 3/16" WIDE
¼" DEEP

⅛" MASONITE

1⅝"x1⅝"x42"

SIDE ELEVATION
SHOWING MASONITE SLIDE
AT REAR

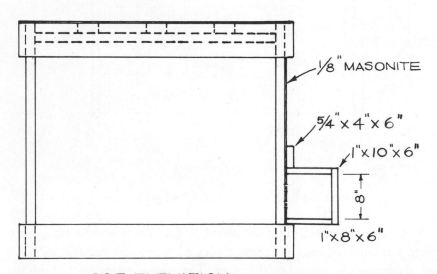

⅛" MASONITE

5/4"x4"x6"

1"x10"x6"

8"

1"x8"x6"

SIDE ELEVATION
SHOWING STATIONARY SLIDE
BACK WITH DUCT ATTACHED FOR VENTILATION

Side elevations of indoor greenhouse.

with No. 12 screws, 2½ inches long, so that the posts will be on the inside of the case. Use three screws at each end of each board. (Depending on where your case is located, you may wish to have glass on three sides and masonite only at the back. Ours was placed in a corner, so only the front and one side were glass.) Under the right lights, you'll get such spectacular results that you will want your plants visible from every angle in the room.

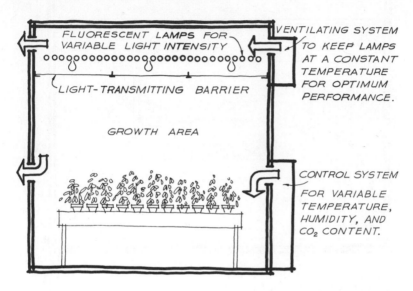

Diagram of growth area, showing where shield should be placed. (*Courtesy General Electric*)

In order to provide a support for the fluorescent fixture, screw a strip of wood 1¾ inches square (obtained by ripping a two-by-four) onto each of the upper two end pieces, 2 inches from the top and fitting closely between the two corner posts. Upon these supports movable two-by-fours, the length of the inside of the case, can rest.

The type of light you are using determines how they are mounted. If you are using a reflector with three or four fluorescent tubes, these are hung with a chain from the two-by-fours. The fixtures weigh over one hundred pounds and require rather heavy construction materials. Power-Groove tubes or slimline fixtures can be mounted directly on the two-by-fours; in fact, two-by-twos are sufficient to support these lamps. To provide ample ventilation, there should be at least an inch of space between the fixtures. If you are using eight tubes, porcelain sockets can be mounted on a two-by-four at spaced intervals to give the needed light, between the fourth and fifth tube. This system of mounting enables you to leave the top open.

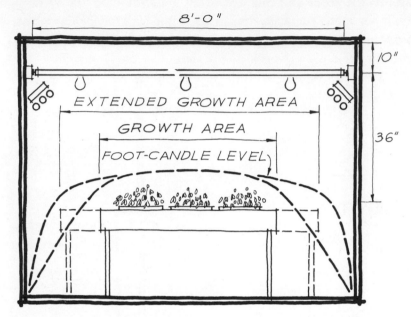

Long view of growth area, showing that higher light intensity is obtained if additional lights are mounted at the side. Dotted lines indicate where light drops off if added lights are not included. (*Courtesy General Electric*)

Between two and four inches below the tubes, the distance depending on the size of your case, screw angle irons on the sides to support the shield. We found that three pieces of glass were easier to handle than a single piece, although with plastic you can use a single sheet in a frame. As heat is always a detriment, the ballasts that operate the tubes should be located outside the case, if at all possible. Otherwise, you may need to cool the case with forced air from the outside. Slide the white masonite boards or sheets of glass into the grooves that you have made in the side supports of the case. Use a masonite board to cover the top by simply resting it on the framework so that it is possible to slide it off if additional ventilation is needed. Since we built our first greenhouse, the use of polyethylene instead of masonite has become understandably widespread. It is easy to install, reasonably priced, and has proved to be an extremely effective substitute.

Two doors with glass panes may be put on hinges at the front. You can make these from ⅝-inch stock, using a rabbet plane to make the notch on which the glass rests. This may be accomplished a little less neatly with strops, by the method explained in the structural directions for the ends and back of the case. The doors, made of ⅝-by-2-inch lumber, are hung with hinges on a piece of wood, of the same dimensions, fastened onto the front of the corner posts between the top and bottom pieces of the case. At the center of the front opening a piece of wood 1 inch by 2 inches is nailed upright to the back of the top and bottom pieces of the case, and in the center of this is nailed another piece, ⅝ by 1⅛ inches, so that the doors will close against the back piece and may be fastened shut with hooks and eyes or latches against the narrower strip.

The base on which the greenhouse rests is simply a strong table. Sturdy legs are made of pieces of wood 2 inches by 3 inches by 20 inches. They may be held together with ⅝-by-6-inch pieces of wood, fastened with No. 12 screws, 3 inches long. To strengthen it further, a 2-by-6-inch piece may be cut the full length of the stand and nailed flat into mortises cut into the center of the 4-foot ends so that the top surface is flush with the tops of the ends. The 4-by-6-foot tabletop may be made of a piece of pressed masonite.

In many situations, instead of resting on a table, the greenhouse can rest on a bench, or even on sawhorses. If it is on sawhorses, a sturdy tabletop support will, of course, have to be made to put under the case. It is also possible to utilize the space beneath for a second case illumined with a second set of lights. When space is at a premium, several tiers may be constructed. The chief disadvantage of this arrangement is that you practically have to lie on your stomach to water the bottom cases. As a result, you are quite likely to find that you are kept so busy caring for those plants at a more convenient height that the lower cases are left almost empty. This arrangement also intensifies the problem of ventilation.

A window at the back of the enclosure is the simplest means of ventilating. In the winter a storm sash needs to be added. In the base of the sash cut a rectangular opening 1½ by 14 inches. If you have room on your sill, you need simply set a piece of wood in front of the opening, and slide it back and forth to open or close it. In cold weather the inner window should be opened only about ⅜ to ½ inch. If there is not room enough to close the opening in this manner, a strip of wood 1 inch thick may be fastened onto the sash with a screw at one end of the opening, so the other end may be raised or lowered. You can also cover the opening by making rabbeted strips at each end, and control the amount of air admitted by sliding a masonite or plywood strip up and down.

More construction is necessary to make a duct for ventilation and controlling the temperature in the indoor greenhouse. It is best made either of plywood or of wood and masonite with an adjustable slide close to your air intake, with which the flow of air is controlled.

The duct can be made by using 1-by-8-inch wood for the top and bottom, and nailing masonite or plywood, 10 inches wide, onto the edges of these two pieces of wood. This gives a nearly square opening on the inside. The duct should be attached along one side of the greenhouse, close to the bottom. To ensure even distribution of the incoming air, 1-inch holes should be drilled through the masonite wall, the entire length of the side. The total area of these holes should not exceed one-half the cross-sectional area of your main air supply.

Connecting the duct to the window requires quite careful fitting, and the way it must be done will differ slightly, depending on the location of the greenhouse in relation to the window from which the air is taken. In general, the easiest way is to remove one of the panes of glass from the window. Make a duct out of 1-inch wood, the end of which fits the windowpane opening, and which will extend inward nine or ten inches beyond the masonry walls. The dimensions vary with the location. The end which extends into the basement is then closed off with masonite, but enough of one side is left open to allow the duct which goes to the greenhouse to join it at right angles. A slide to control the amount of air which enters is made of ⅛-inch masonite to fit into a slot where the intake duct and the duct to the greenhouse meet. In cold weather the slide is pulled out just a little way; in the spring and fall you may need to remove it entirely, as well as to place a small electric fan in the opening in the window to force the air inside.

Occasionally the trouble that one faces with an indoor greenhouse is that a large part of the year it is too cold rather than too warm. The case will then need to be insulated with a wall of double thickness made from two pieces of masonite. Possibly at night, when the lamps are turned out, you will need to have additional heat. Small heating units can be screwed into ordinary light sockets. Sometimes you may need to mount two or three in series. The temperature will then need to be controlled with an air thermostat. These simple devices for temperature control work well when it is cold, but are inadequate during the hot summer months. One must either keep the plants out of doors, or install an automatic temperature control. In schools, where there is no one around during the weekend, and in warmer climates, it is a year-round necessity.

Francis C. Hall, whose geranium doll house we discussed in Chapter 4, has an excellent arrangement. At the base of his greenhouse he in-

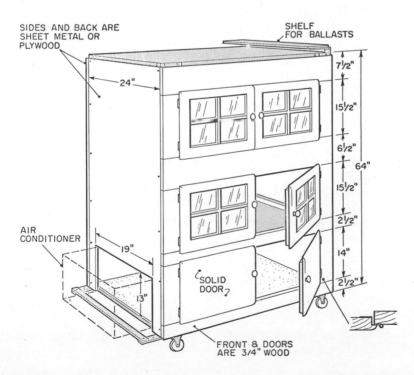

Francis C. Hall's geranium doll house with its air conditioner. (*Courtesy Francis C. Hall*)

stalled a small air conditioner like those used in windows. It is placed with the front end inside and the warm-air discharge outside. Through bypassing the regular thermostat and wiring the air conditioner to a Honeywell air switch, he can be sure that the temperature in his indoor greenhouse will vary by only three degrees. In addition to a device for controlling temperature, you may also want to install instruments to measure the relative humidity and the amount of carbon dioxide in the air. These are inexpensive and not difficult to obtain.

The delightful part of gardening under lights is that simple devices and elaborate ones both have their place. Whatever type of greenhouse you finally decide to build, you are on the threshold of a new experience. It may be as simple as one plant under an incandescent bulb or as elaborate as a growth chamber, but it leads to new and unexplored paths. Gardening is always exciting, but digging in the dirt and growing flowers while the snow piles up in the back yard is poignantly new and challenging.

 *13*

AID FOR THE
WINDOW GARDEN

As we have already pointed out, lamplight combined with window light is a Prince Charming for almost anything that is being grown in the house. Relatively small amounts of artificial rays will change the appearance of almost any windowsill plant, and bring about the complete transformation of many.

The most startling experience we had was when our jade tree, *Crassula arborescens*, suddenly blossomed. For a number of years we had more or less tolerated it on the windowsill. It had ceased to be an upright stalk with fleshy leaves, gradually taking on the appearance of a small tree with stems an inch thick and a slightly picturesque, gnarled habit of growth that had kept us from throwing it out. But with just 50 foot-candles more light from a 60-watt incandescent bulb, there began to appear on small cymes early in the winter literally hundreds of tiny pinkish-white buds.

As with Cinderella, everyone stopped to admire. Beautiful as the buds were, the flowers were still lovelier. They had a foamy delicate appearance, and they covered the leaves as cherry blossoms conceal the branches of the tree. The blossoms were not merely a passing phenomenon but lasted from six to eight weeks, and even their passing was marked with elegance.

Such a performance makes the jade tree worth coddling. It needs a pot five to six inches in diameter, the soil given in the recipe in Chapter 16, and, while the buds are forming, a light intensity of at least 300 foot-candles. To make sure we will not be disappointed, we grow it for a few months in our lamplight greenhouse and then return it to the windowsill to blossom.

The shrimp plant, too, became a thing of beauty on our windowsill with a small amount of added radiance from the electric bulb. Its bracts, each one of which lasts from four to five weeks, blend from dark orange to a light yellow suffused with crimson. There were always a few of these bracts that hung on long after its fleeting white flowers disappeared, without the aid of additional light. But the added light made it blossom so magnificently that we felt the name "shrimp plant" somewhat lacking in imagination. It is said to have received this name because the flushed bracts reminded some hungry horticulturist of boiled shrimp. Actually, its botanical name, *Beloperone guttata*, is more fitting.

The growth of only a single plant, the Christmas cactus (*Zygocactus truncatus*) was disrupted by additional light. Ours had grown quite successfully on the windowsill for a number of years, but when more light was added it did not blossom. We put it in a dark corner of the veranda during a large part of a cold, rainy August and September. When we finally looked at it, the few remaining sprigs were covered with buds.

This was a vivid demonstration that the Christmas cactus is a short-day plant, a fact that makes it possible to produce blossoms at almost any time of the year by adjusting the light to suit it. It also explains why plants blossom on different windowsills between Thanksgiving and Easter. If your windowsill plant does not blossom in winter, it may be that your living-room lights are making its day too long. Cover it from dinnertime till morning with a black cloth for six or eight weeks, and it will reward you with showers of its beautiful red blossoms.

Your windowsills can also be improved if you grow plants in your indoor greenhouse for a while and then promote them to the living-room window. In fact, you soon discover that they add such charm that, if only to increase the attractiveness of your home, it is well worth devoting a portion of your indoor greenhouse to the growing of foliage plants.

Nothing is as inexpensive as sunlight, but when sunlight is lacking the wise indoor gardener makes up for its deficiency by using artificial illumination. In supplementing window light, you can use incandescent bulbs, fluorescent tubes, or both together. Of course, when houses are crowded closely together, the windowsills receive only a small amount of light. The plants in the window are then growing largely under artificial light.

There is another use of lamplight which you might overlook. By the judicious placing of a lamp you can keep the plants on your windowsill from turning their backs on you. Their leaves, instead of reaching toward the windows, will respond quickly to the more intense light from the lamp, and the results are lovelier. Scientists point out that the *dark* side of any stem elongates, which gives the effect of leaves reaching toward the light.

WHAT TO DO

COME SUMMER

One's interest in lamplight gardening does not exactly wane in the summer; it is just pushed out of mind by the glory of plenty of natural light, an abundance of flowers, and being able to sit in the sun with a glass of cold lemonade, watching nature do all the work. But after you have nourished a plant all winter your conscience will not let it die, even though its charm may be greater for you in December than in June.

The light that you get through most windows in the summer is greater in intensity than any that your best-balanced arrangement of fluorescent tubes and incandescent bulbs can provide. This fact suggests one way out: you can put all your plants on the windowsill and let them enjoy the benefits of long summer days and warm air currents. Of course you can also leave them under the artificial lights and get the same fine results you got in winter. However, summer diversions may keep you from giving your plants the undivided attention you gave them during the dark, cheerless winter months. In that event, you may decide to take a holiday from intensive window gardening and move your plants about so that your only task will be to water them.

You will like your plants better if you can employ them outside for decorative effects. Finding the right use to put them to may call for a little imagination. A humble home on a shaded street well illustrated to us and to all who passed by what could be done with houseplants out of doors. On the side of a small cement stoop, which was scarcely more than twenty feet from the sidewalk, a wooden lattice was constructed to protect the plants from the wind. Against this shelter an old plant stand made a living wall of green. Other plants hung in baskets; still others, in colorfully decorated pots, lined the sidewalk. All winter long no one would give this house a second glance; in the summer everyone stopped to look and admire.

Any outdoor living area, whether it be a veranda, a terrace, or a screened porch that faces north, is very much to a plant's liking. Porches facing south, east, or west are quite suitable for houseplants as long as there is plenty of shade; but few houseplants will grow well if they are taken out of the relative darkness of artificial lighting and plunged into the intensity of the rays of the midday sun. Early-morning or late-afternoon sunshine may strike them without any damage.

Ivies or philodendron may trail over the sides of the windowbox and, using ferns and other plants as a background for pots of tuberous-rooted begonias, you will make the shady side of your house as lovely as the sunny side, where petunias run riot in gay colors. Of course your plants must be watered, no matter where you put them, but you can use the hose in the evening when the water in the pipes is still warm.

Difficulties arise when you leave home for the summer, or even for two weeks. Your plants are like the dog or cat that you cannot take with you but do not like to leave behind. If you are to be gone for only two weeks and have no one to care for your plants, the best solution is to place the plants in a box which has small drainage holes and is off the ground in a shady spot. Fill the box with peat moss and rig up a shield of plastic to protect the plants from heavy rains. Lathes make a good covering material since they admit water but keep off the full force of the rain. Soak the peat moss and the plants thoroughly before you go, and try to find someone who will water them occasionally until you return. Even if he forgets, your plants will survive.

Another successful system is to establish the plants in self-watering pans with a somewhat deeper water level than is used indoors. Watering the plants thus becomes such a simple operation that you can probably find a friend or a handyman who will care for them till you return.

You might prefer to give your plants to your friends who are staying in town for the summer, giving them also the right to gather a slip or two in the fall—or, better still, to make a few slips for you and care for them. In the fall the slips will be excellent young plants.

Despite this good counsel, we follow it only in part. We find that giving away our plants is too much like parting with our own children. So we take slips and take our plants with us too, under circumstances which, to put it mildly, are difficult.

We own and operate a summer camp for children, and in the springtime our minds are filled with children—not plants. But at the very moment when a mother is calling to ask, "How many blankets do you need in the woods?" and the second cook has decided she cannot come after all, the plants must be packed up in boxes, watered, and stored away to await the first calm, cloudy day. Then we put them in the truck and carry them off to camp.

Everyone is now too busy to care, but there they are, grouped on benches around trees, stuck into windowboxes, and waiting to be watered. A few of our darlings and our new cuttings are installed under lights.

Before long they all emerge from their anonymity and insist on showing their colors as beautifully as they did at home under artificial lights. The African violets continue to bloom luxuriantly; the begonias put out their bright blossoms; and finally even the children stop playing to admire them. "Those are pretty flowers," they comment, and even the severe, though friendly, critics of nature must admit that houseplants adjust very well to the woods.

For many years we were deceived by the pleasant, golden warmth of September in western New York, and left our plants out of doors. But a cold, hard rain, a couple of clear, beautiful nights, and our plants would begin to deteriorate. We well remember how a freak hailstorm was the death-knell to our African violets. In spite of our tenderest care thereafter, practically none of them recovered, and even leaves taken to propagate new plants failed to root. Most houseplants are very susceptible to temperatures below 40 degrees Fahrenheit, even if they are exposed to the cold for only a short time. The safe practice is to turn on your lights in your lamplight greenhouse early in September and to place your plants beneath them.

🌼 Come Fall

Gathering the plants together under one roof is the beginning of spring for indoor gardeners. There is the same throbbing sensation of life unfolding as when the first annuals are planted while the phoebe bobs its tail and sings. So much waits to be done. The coleus is far too lanky and must be lopped off; the prayer plant has completely outgrown its pot; and those rooted leaves of the amazing new African violet (there is *always* a *new* African violet) are ready to be potted.

Any plant that has spent the summer out of doors is liable to be host to unwelcome guests, especially to earthworms. These night crawlers may be of value in the garden, but definitely not in a flowerpot. In a tiny pot they honeycomb the soil with canals which fill with water; this excess moisture prevents the proper amount of oxygen from reaching the roots of the plants, and without sufficient oxygen the plants will ultimately stop growing. Fortunately, earthworms are easy to get rid of. Just knock the plant out of the pot and immerse the ball of earth in water; the worms will emerge in a very short time.

Another precaution to take when your plants are brought indoors is to give them a thorough syringing. Syringing, though not a cure-all, is a good precaution against insects. We hold the plants sideways over a tub or the sink and wash them gently with a spray of lukewarm water. There may be a few aphids or some mealy bugs on the coleus but in general, keeping plants out of doors in the summer does not necessarily mean an influx of pests. Some may need a spray of insecticide; a few may have to be discarded. But it does not matter—a winter of good gardening lies ahead.

❀ ✳ ❧ ❀ ❀ ✳ *15*

LAMPS FOR THE

OUTDOOR GARDEN

The artificial suns, fluorescent tubes and incandescent bulbs, are slowly moving outdoors. What they achieved indoors is being repeated in florists' fields, in outdoor gardens, and even in the conventional outdoor greenhouses.

The importance of the use of artificial lights has been indirectly recognized in outdoor gardens for some time. There has been no question about the superiority of seedlings grown under lights. Gardeners have found that from these seedlings they can harvest tomatoes, lettuce, cabbages, cucumbers, and melons much earlier in the season. Flowers will blossom a month earlier than usual, in full summer glory. (See Chapter 22.)

But there is also direct recognition of the importance of using lights in gardening out of doors. Florists often string lights about twelve feet apart, six feet from the ground, over the plants growing beneath them. Incandescent bulbs are becoming an accepted part of professional growers' greenhouses. Even amateurs who do not care to grow plants indoors but prefer small outdoor greenhouses are finding them useful. It is important for gardeners to understand the proper manipulation of the intensity, duration, and quality of light as it holds such meaningful possibilities for the outdoor garden.

Florists who have put artificial lighting in greenhouses have proved how commercially effective the knowledge of photoperiodism may be. One grower was facing a considerable loss because his Easter lilies were far behind schedule. In desperation he installed fluorescent lamps in his greenhouse and left them turned on half the night. Ten days before Easter, in spite of his efforts, there seemed to be little hope that the tight green buds would swell and burst into bloom. But he had miscalculated the powerful effects of additional artificial light. Two days before Easter Sunday enough buds had opened to make every plant salable.

Lights can also be used to postpone the blossoming of plants. Chrysanthemums, poinsettias, and daisies, which are all short-day plants, can be brought into bloom as late as Christmas instead of October or November when they normally flower. Since they need long nights in order to bloom, turning on lights of relatively low intensity (30 foot-candles) even for a few minutes will give the effect of a short night. Instead of producing flowers, the plants will get bushy and grow leaves. If the lights are connected to a timer so that they can be turned on for ten minutes and off for fifty, then on again for ten and off for fifty, the blossoming time of any short-day plant is controlled. The rhythmic turning on and off of the lights is known as cyclic lighting. As soon as the plants are given long nights after this treatment, they will flower.

The effect on plants of both long and short days, as well as the quality of light, is one of the studies that plant physiologists consider important. It is being investigated in colleges, universities, and phytotrons all over the world. (See also Chapter 24.) Photocontrol of plant behavior is more complex than it appears and is not solved simply by adjusting time switches. For one thing, we know that the ratio of far-red to red light is very important to plant behavior, but much study is still needed to understand its effects fully.

The incandescent lamp that is usually used out of doors is the PS 30 reflectorized bulb, which, because of its shape, does not have the hot spot characteristic of some incandescent bulbs. The 150- and 250-watt sizes of this bulb cover four times as much area as does a standard 100-watt bulb in a garden. These lights make it possible to illuminate an average outdoor garden with relatively few lamps. They need to be protected from rain or snow with a suitable reflector, as they have soft glass bulbs which may break when exposed to moisture.

As we have pointed out, the study of photoperiodism is still such a new field that one who is experimentally minded can greatly enjoy working in his garden with these lights. Much work has been done in checking and rechecking the response of flowering plants to day-lengths, but the more subtle conditions affecting their growth are still open questions. Some of these questions started a doctor friend investigating the effects of light on plants out of doors. Before he knew it, he was an enthusiastic indoor lamplight gardener as well.

You may not always wish to hold back or encourage the flowering times of certain plants, but if there is a birthday for which you would like to have the best and fullest bloom, an exhibition at a county fair, or a local garden show that you want to enter, you can easily use the methods that the florists do. If you center 100-watt lights in a twelve-by-fourteen-foot square, six feet above the ground, you will have sufficient illumination to make your short-day plants slow down on flowering. It used to take four hours of illumination to make the night short, but you will find cyclic lighting—as described above—just as effective.

You are probably much more interested in encouraging plants to flower as quickly as possible. Oftentimes a small amount of light will be enough. Outside one of our picture windows one year we had planted a bed of China asters. Indoors, under a valance at the top of the window, we had two fluorescent lamps which lighted some special begonias we had in the window and also the asters outside. Quite often the lights were on until midnight. To our surprise, the asters budded in late June and blossomed in early July. We attributed the precociousness chiefly to the early spring. Eventually, we discovered that it had been due to the lights. We later found that just 10 additional foot-candles of light at the beginning and end of a sunny day would make the China aster blossom far ahead of its normal flowering time.

Until recently, lighting out of doors was used mainly to enhance the beauty of the outdoor garden, but as people come to realize the effects that even small amounts of light have on garden plants, they are using fluorescent and incandescent lamps increasingly.

One of the most spectacular examples that we have seen was the effect of incandescent lamps on the growth of shrub cuttings. Part of a friend's garden was to be bulldozed away to make room for a new highway. This was in August, close to the end of the growing season in western New York State. Our friend, undaunted, cut off the tops of the shrubs, making each cutting two or three feet long. He planted these tops together in large bunches in big holes that he had previously dug and filled with peat moss. He used between six and eight incandescent lamps to floodlight the rows of shrubs. He carefully watered the peat moss so that it was always damp. When the snow came in late November, he turned off the lights and stopped watering. The following spring and summer the shrubs blossomed. The transplanted forsythia, flowering quince, flowering almond, philadelphus, and rose-of-Sharon bloomed beautifully, not as struggling new bushes but as well-established shrubs.

The study of day-lengths is a new field. You may be able to contribute new knowledge of value to outdoor gardeners everywhere. At any rate, you will enjoy the beauty of your flowers.

PART III

*Cultural Directions
for Growing Plants
under Lights*

THE SOIL RECIPE

You may have a fine installation of lights, good ventilation, and a means of controlling temperature, yet be greatly disappointed in the plants you grow. Unless their roots are well anchored in a good soil, all your plants, from the smallest annual to the largest begonia you can squeeze under your greenhouse lights, will grow poorly.

All good gardeners know that soil must be carefully mixed, porous and well drained, rich in humus and fertilizer. Out of doors we dig in sand and ashes, leafmold, rotted manure, and peat moss. But if you dig and poke in a flowerpot, adding a little of this and a little of that, you can be quite devastating to your vegetables, annuals, and houseplants.

We well remember the year we transplanted our tiny seedlings into some self-fertilizing paper pots that, according to the assurances of our gardening friends, would give us vegetables that looked better than the pictures in the catalogs. But just that extra fertility, together with the soil we were then using for our seedlings, was too much of a good thing. We practically killed off our vegetables and flowers with too much kindness.

Finding the right kind of soil for our seedlings, as well as for the plants in our lamplight greenhouse, was a long, long process, made possible only because of the vigor with which plants grew under artificial lights. Again and again the effect of relatively small changes in our potting soil was graphically illustrated to us. For instance, when we potted fourteen plantlets from the same parent propagating leaf of an African violet in fourteen different soil mixtures, and placed them under the same set of lights, each plant grew differently. Some quickly sent up new leaves, some remained practically stationary, some grew for a time and then withered away, and one actually sent up a flower stem when it had only a few leaves.

The growth of three Christmas begonia cuttings, quite similar and all the same size, indicated that, if anything, begonias were even more susceptible to the changing of a few teaspoonfuls of material. One grew about two inches tall in three months' time; the second measured five or six inches across and boasted two flower stems; while the third was a full foot in diameter and covered with blooms. Our search for a superior soil, compatible with both seedlings and houseplants, began long before we knew anything about lamplight gardening, and has continued ever since.

We remember asking a friend during those early years, "Where do you get your soil?" for her plants were as luxuriant in January as ours in midsummer.

Her answer almost made us country-dwellers. "Oh, I just dig it up behind the barn," she said. Lacking the barn with good dirt behind it, we had to learn to make our own.

Horticultural literature is rich in suggestions, but invariably lacks precision, or it recommends materials that vary greatly in consistency. In addition, many are impossible for the apartment-dweller or the suburbanite to obtain. Often the recipes are like those of a great chef and can be duplicated only by the originators. In fact, many times we found it well-nigh impossible to reproduce some of our own creations.

The soil formula we were seeking was one that would give a loose-textured mixture, which over a long period of time did not pack together, which under the dry conditions of the home retained sufficient moisture, and in which plants would grow well not only for a few months but, if necessary, for several years.

Here is the recipe we evolved and the reasoning back of it:

❀ The Recipe

> *4 cups of soil*
> *5 cups of peat moss*
> *4 cups coarse vermiculite*
> *5 teaspoonfuls whiting*

❀ The Materials

Soil. Dirt is dirt only to the housewife, never to a gardener. It makes a considerable difference both in a flowerpot and in a garden whether you start with garden loam or sand or sticky clay. This can be readily verified by those who have tried raising plants in newly excavated subsoil or in almost pure sand that surrounds cottages at the seashore. A heavy clay soil is not desirable, for it is virtually impossible to make it porous, and a sandy soil is usually unsatisfactory because it contains so little clay. It is easy enough to recognize these two types of soil, but it is somewhat harder for a beginner to know a heavy silt loam when he sees it, and that is the most desirable soil for your flowerpots.

An excellent means of identifying it was pointed out to us by five-year-old Mary Lou. "You need good dirt to make good mud pies," she explained to us in a voice that clearly imitated a cooking expert on television. "It has to stick together," she said as she carefully added water to the mixture and patted it into a cake about a quarter of an inch thick. "But when you bend it, it should break," she continued, taking up one of her freshly made mud pies and breaking it up into "delicious pieces" for her doll.

We examined one of the pieces and marveled at how right she was. We were thinking in terms not of dolls but of our own pet project. To Mary Lou's delight, we sat down beside her and joined in making mud pies. We tried some pies from dirt that was almost clay. Mary Lou picked them up and bent them, but they would not break into doll-sized pieces. "It's not good dirt," she remarked. She was right. It was not good dirt for houseplants, either, since it contained too much finely divided clay.

She was just as emphatic about some rather sandy soil that one of us suggested we use. The mud pies were gritty and crumbled in our hands. Mary Lou's pigtails swung as she shook her head. "You see, it's not good dirt," she emphasized. "You have to be careful when you're mixing these things."

The mud-pie method is an excellent test for the soil you plan to use. Suitable soil sticks together when you pick up a "pie" and breaks when you bend it. The test means nothing, however, if you are a poor mud-pie maker and add too much water.

Of course, you can also tell something about the soil by rubbing it in your hands when it is dry. If it has a gritty feeling between your fingers, it is sandy; if it feels floury, it is silt; and if the lumpy particles are harsh to the touch, it is clay. A silt loam also becomes somewhat lumpy as it dries, but these lumps break up easily between the fingers. The higher the clay content of the soil, the more difficult it is to break up the lumps. In looking for a soil, choose one that, when *completely dry*, varies in shade from light tan to brownish-black. The color varies, depending on the amount of humus in the soil. A slight amount of moisture will greatly change the color tone and make the test worthless. Soils that are red or black in color should be viewed with caution. Some soils are black because they contain leafmold, but many soils that are black when dry consist chiefly of sand and a small amount of organic material. In western New York such soil is quite common. It is usually gathered from bogs and is quite unsuitable for growing plants. Red soil, on the other hand, is likely to be pure clay.

Fortunately, there is plenty of good soil available throughout the United States. Garden soil is excellent to use as a foundation. Perhaps a friend will give you some from his garden if you have no garden of your own. Good soil can also be found in fields. If you dig some there, be sure to take it from a place where the vegetation is rank, and use only the top two or three inches. Many times an excellent soil can be found along river and creek banks, where a heavy silt loam has been deposited. Throughout the world this has proved to be superb for growing things. Florists, nurserymen, and plant departments also sell dirt which is generally suitable for use in this recipe.

During the many years we were experimenting intensively with growing plants under artificial lights, the soil used in our recipe was collected from quite different sources, but their one point of similarity was that *all* were heavy silt loam. We found, and it seemed surprising to us at first, that when *mixed in the proper proportions* with the other substances given in this recipe, the source of the silt loam made very little difference.

Peat Moss. The second ingredient needed for your soil mixture is peat moss. Ordinary garden peat can be used, such as is usually sold in bales, but it should be screened to get rid of the large lumps. It can also be purchased, usually screened, in smaller amounts from the florist and at plant counters.

We prefer the peat moss that comes from West Germany. When it is screened, it produces particles that remind you of frayed thread rather than lumps. This texture makes for a firmer soil.

The real danger in buying either German or Canadian peat moss is getting a bale that has been kept wet for some time. This makes the peat moss extremely acid, and it is very difficult to wash it out. One way of testing whether it has been kept wet is to look at the containers. German peat moss is shipped in burlap, and if the burlap is in good condition you can be sure it has not been kept wet. Canadian peat is shipped in paper or paper cartons, and it too is often very good. Canadian peat, however, tends to be more acid than German peat, and is quite finely broken up so that it can plug airholes in a potting mixture. If you sift it and do not use any of the fine material you can use it safely.

Vermiculites. Vermiculite is a completely inert material, a form of mica that has been heated to make it porous and spongelike. There are several grades, but the one you want is known as Number One, Insulating Vermiculite. It contains the largest particles.

In addition to its wonderful spongelike quality, which enables it to hold so much water, vermiculite serves to keep the soil porous. Sand is often used to increase porosity in the soil, but the dual function of vermiculite makes it more useful in a soil mixture.

Whiting. Whiting is a form of ground limestone, and its chemical properties are therefore those of limestone. However, in a soil mixture whiting is more effective than other ground limestone because the particles are much smaller. In texture and appearance it resembles flour. It is easy to understand why a flourlike substance mixes better than one consisting of small pellets. Whiting can be purchased in most hardware and paint stores, and at some plant counters.

If whiting is not available, it is permissible to use ground limestone, but not dehydrated lime. Lime, too, is a white powder which contains calcium, but the resemblance ends right there. Used in the potting soil in the proportions given for whiting, it would make your soil alkaline, with a pH of 10.0 or over, and your plants would not survive.

Scientists have developed a numerical system to specify the range of acidity or alkalinity, and the descriptive symbol written before the number to designate this is pH. A pH of 7.0 is neutral, but for practical purposes a soil with a pH between 6.8 and 7.2 is considered virtually neutral. The lower the pH reading, the more acid a soil contains.

Soil becomes more and more acid through the decaying of organic materials, which form dilute acids, including carbonic acid. In a soil mixture where so much peat moss is used, it is necessary to neutralize these acids, except for plants that prefer to grow in an acid soil. The list of acid-loving plants is not long, compared with those which grow better in a soil that is practically neutral. For three years we experimented with the two types of soil, one kept neutral by the addition of whiting, and the other kept slightly acid. All annuals, perennials, vegetables, and houseplants were grown in both types under the same conditions. Rarely were the plants grown in acid soil as healthy and vigorous as those grown in neutral soil. Seedlings, especially, like a neutral soil. In an acid soil they very shortly stopped growing; their leaves became yellow and in many cases disappeared altogether.

Moreover, if one starts with a soil mixture that is slightly acid, even one as high as pH 6.7, the decomposition of humus within the soil will soon make it excessively acid. This is especially likely when peat moss is used as humus. We were surprised to find that two of our star begonias which had completely stopped growing were in soils which tested pH 6.5 and pH 6.1, respectively. We made exhaustive chemical tests on both of these soils to determine whether they contained nutrients in the right amounts to encourage proper growth. We found that the nutrients were there in the correct proportions—the only deterrent was the acidity of the soil. The soils were neutralized by running lime water through them, and growth began again. Lime water does not, of course, keep a soil permanently neutral; when the soils again became acid, the growth of the plants was halted once more.

It is conceivable that plants might thrive in a soil very slightly acid, were there a means of keeping it so. To attempt to would require constant accurate testing. This is possible only with a *p*H meter, a very expensive electronic instrument. Certain kits for testing soil acidity are on the market, but we have found it difficult to interpret accurately the results they give. Color charts are furnished with these kits, and different hues indicate degrees of acidity. The *p*H, or acidity of the soil, is determined by comparing the color of the solution, in which a sample of soil has been mixed, with the shade of color on the master chart. However, the shade of the test solution is considerably affected by the clay content of the soil. This causes various soils to produce different shades in the test solution, even though the acid content may be the same.

You can eliminate the necessity of struggling with these *p*H kits, and grow better plants as well, by mixing enough whiting into the soil to make certain that it remains neutral. The whiting must be thoroughly worked throughout the entire mixture so that there will be no pockets where acids can form.

Some plants, of course, prefer an acid soil. You mix an acid soil by merely omitting the whiting from the recipe. Philodendron, grape ivy, some of the gesneriads, azaleas, and many orchids are acid-loving plants. (Orchids, however, will not grow in this soil mixture but need special materials. See Chapter 27.) Many of the acid-loving plants need a very open mixture, and most of them grow better in the soil recipe with half of the vermiculite replaced by charcoal, and no whiting.

❋ Utensils Needed

Mixing Bowl or Washbasin. We found the washbasin somewhat better because of the rounded bottom and the shallow sides. This makes it easier to mix the materials thoroughly.

Baking Dish. A large-sized turkey roaster will hold ½ bushel of soil. However, a pan that holds 3 quarts will be large enough for this recipe.

Screen Made of Hardware Cloth. A screen for sifting both dirt and peat moss may be made from white pine strips, ¾ inch thick and 2 to 3 inches wide. The boards are cut square at the ends and nailed together to form a square or rectangle. Strips 12 to 14 inches in length make a convenient size. No. 6 box nails should be used in nailing the frame together. A 4- or 6-mesh hardware cloth is tacked on with No. 6 carpet staples. A 6-mesh cloth is *much* better, but harder to find. To protect yourself from the sharp edges of the wire, nail a thin strip of wood over the edges of the hardware cloth. These strips should be ¾ inch in width and about ½ inch thick. They can be nailed on with No. 3 or No. 4 box nails.

❀ *Procedure*

1. Carefully measure the materials into the mixing bowl in the order given. This leaves the vermiculite and the whiting on top.

2. With your fingers mix the materials together until the mixture is uniform in texture.

3. Add a small amount of water, perhaps ½ cup, depending on the dryness of the loam; add enough water to keep it from dusting.

4. Rub the materials together with the palms of your hands, or push them through the screen. Mixing the various substances into a smooth-textured mass is easier when you employ the hardware-cloth screen. When you have a particularly claylike soil, you may have to push it through the screen four or five times in order to integrate the peat moss and the soil particles. If you work with small amounts, such as are given in the recipe, the loam that results from this mixing process will please the most seasoned gardener.

5. Sterilizing the soil is the next step after the loam is mixed. Do not use it for your plants before sterilizing. Put the soil in the baking dish and pour sufficient water over it to wet it thoroughly. You can make sure that the water has penetrated by cutting through the mixture with a spoon or a knife. When you press your hand down on the soil, water should ooze up between your fingers.

Preheat the oven to 275 degrees Fahrenheit, place the pan of soil in it, and bake it for an hour. The soil is well sterilized when the top begins to cake and the mass is steaming.

6. Allow the soil to dry out until the surface is light in color and the mass cracks. It can then be easily screened by pushing it through

the hardware cloth. This final screening makes the texture light and fluffy, and the volume will be nearly doubled.

7. Store the sterilized soil anywhere except on the ground, where pests can walk into it. Sometimes objections are raised to sterilizing soil by people who cry, "It kills the bacteria." They are right—it does, but there are enough bacteria around to make up the deficit immediately. We have transplanted innumerable cuttings, seedlings, and larger plants into soil that was just cool from the oven. They have grown as well as plants placed in soil that was sterilized more than a year earlier.

Some people have tried sterilizing soil in their ovens and given it up because they "just couldn't stand the smell." You have a smell *only if you do not thoroughly wet your soil*. Whatever you are sterilizing must be wet all the way through, with some water standing on top. The conversion of this water into steam is what does so effective a job of sterilizing.

Just at the end there will be a slight odor, but it is not objectionable. It is something like a caramel smell, and disappears immediately. Besides, if you have wet your materials thoroughly, you can take the pan out of the oven as soon as the odor becomes noticeable.

❀ Amount

This recipe makes about 3 quarts of potting soil. For most lamplight gardening this amount will last for a long time.

❀ Large-Scale Mixture

The fun of growing plants under lights invariably results in the acquisition of more plants and the need for more potting soil. It is not practical to make up a large quantity unless you are planning to use it immediately, for once the full amounts of peat moss and vermiculite have been added, they gradually settle out, so the soil has to be mixed again.

The best method is to sterilize separately ½ bushel of soil and ½ bushel of peat moss. Then you will always have ready the materials you need for mixing up a batch of soil. The vermiculite does not need to be sterilized. The same method is used in sterilizing both the soil and the peat moss. Wet thoroughly, place ½ bushel in a large pan, and bake in a preheated oven at 275 degrees Fahrenheit for 1½ hours. Let the soil or peat moss dry out until you are able to screen it. Screen, allow to dry out completely, and store off the ground.

SOILLESS MIXTURES
AND HUMUS

Of making of mixtures for growing plants there shall be no end. We have only to look at our notes! For years, Soil Mixture 52 grew beautiful plants for us and for thousands of others, but today, it seems that Soul Mixture 69 (which is the one given in this book) does a better job. So, the search goes on. As soon as you grow plants under lights and talk with your friends about what they are growing, you will find yourself experimenting with your own mixtures. At present, we are experimenting with Soil Mixture 101, which has no soil in it at all. Soilless mixtures are an important part of the modern trend.

Cornell University has worked out several soils of this type. Their "instant soil" was developed by Professors R. Sheldrake and J. Boodley, researchers in the Departments of Vegetable Crops and Floriculture. You actually do not need to mix it yourself for it is sold commercially under the name of Jiffy-Mix. However, those with an experimental interest will want to know what goes into this modern substitute for soil. Their recipe is as follows:

	One-peck mix	One-bushel mix
Vermiculite—No. 2 size	4 quarts	½ bushel
Shredded peat moss	4 quarts	½ bushel

	One-peck mix	*One-bushel mix*
Powdered limestone (whiting)	1 tablespoon	4 tablespoons
Superphosphate 20	1 teaspoon	1 tablespoon
Fertilizer (5 parts nitrogen, 10 parts phosphorus, 5 parts potassium)	2–4 teaspoons	8–16 teaspoons

The commercial Jiffy-Mix is quite uniform, and strenuous efforts are made to keep it so. It is a real boon to city-dwellers and to gardeners everywhere who hate to take the time to mix their own soil. It is even used in phytotrons. To many the soil comes as a revelation. It scarcely seems possible that plants will grow very well, indeed, not only without soil, but without the special kinds of humus that have been the byword of good gardeners for generations: leafmold and rotted manure.

"Humus" is the word all gardeners roll off their tongues appreciatively, for the substances it describes are essential to the luxuriant growth of all plants, substances which are derived from decayed vegetation and decayed refuse from animals. Peat moss, rotted manure, and leafmold are the most familiar forms. Their names are practically garden passwords, and to the plants they are almost life itself.

Actually there are not too many plants that justify mixing a soil containing these products. The gardenia, the camellia, and some of the other broad-leafed evergreens like a leafmold mixture very well.

Peat moss is so easily available commercially that it has pretty well crowded out other forms of humus, but gardeners should know the advantages and disadvantages of the other types, so that they may use them wisely if they have a sudden windfall.

We found that the soil for which the recipe is given in the preceding chapter becomes quite acid when no whiting is added. In many pots it tested close to pH 4.0. The leafmold soil, on the other hand, rarely tested below pH 5.0, and in most pots we found it had a pH of 5.5.

In mixing a leafmold soil, we discovered that it is essential to add some peat moss. Soil in which leafmold is the only form of humus loses its excellent quality by degrees. Within six to eight months, the leafmold disintegrates, leaving only the mineral substances, which do not add to the porosity of the soil. The soil is no longer loose and packs together.

We have mixed and used many different leafmold soils, but in the recipe given here plants grew extremely well.

❀ *Leafmold Soil Mixture*

> *4 cups silt loam*
> *2 cups peat moss*
> *2 cups leafmold*
> *2 cups vermiculite*
> *6 teaspoonfuls whiting (omit if acid soil is desired)*

Mix and sterilize the materials. Then dry, cool, and screen after sterilizing.

❀ *Leafmold*

Leafmold is the decayed vegetable matter of fallen leaves, and is rich in minerals which have already been absorbed through the roots of trees. Although billions of leaves fall and decay each year, leafmold is a rare substance. While it has been gathered successfully by some, our experience impels us to advise against just digging up leafmold in the woods. Sometimes it is excellent, but more often you gather a type that contains ingredients harmful to plants. In our northern forests, deciduous trees, hemlock, and pine grow in the same woods. Leafmold gathered in these woods may contain oils from the decayed evergreen needles, which is the Socrates cup to any plant.

We can remember the half-bushel of leafmold we brought home— nice black humus that had accumulated around the stump of a birch tree. It appeared to be the last word in leafmold; however, when we used it in soil, our houseplants died off one by one, except for a single grape ivy. This flourished for three years or more, as if to disprove our theory by its very vitality. But suddenly, one day, its leaves began to dry up and fall off. When we looked for its roots, we found they had disappeared.

Preparation. Although it is unwise to gather leafmold, and it can seldom be purchased, you can make it. You need patience as well as leaves, however, and something to keep the leaves in place. We hold them down with tree branches, but, if space is at a premium, the leaves can be held down by a frame covered with a wire-mesh screen. The frame rests on the ground and can be of any size—the only important dimension is the height. The enclosure should be from 3½ to 4 feet tall.

Pack the leaves firmly into your frame and wet them down. The leaves should be kept moist at all times to encourage decomposition. Turn the pile of leaves over every two or three months if the weather permits. The mass of leaves will shrink markedly during the warm weather as decomposition continues. It is unlikely that a large amount of leafmold will be formed the first year, but by the end of the second summer you will have a black mass of fertile humus in which the leaf structure is no longer visible. You will be proud of it because you made it. Leafmold made in this manner will contain from 45 to 55 per cent of mineral substances.

As soon as the leafmold is ready, gather it and let it dry out. If it is permitted to stay wet, it will continue to disintegrate and, finally, almost disappear. Before you use your leafmold, it must be screened, sterilized, allowed to dry, and screened again. It takes from 25 to 35 bushels of leaves to make 1 bushel of leafmold. A bushel of leafmold is enough for 5 bushels of potting soil.

Some gardeners recommend adding ½ pound of finely ground limestone to a bushel of firmly packed leaves in order to speed up the disintegration process. We tried this and found it did not perceptibly shorten the time required to make leafmold. Moreover, the method has several disadvantages. It is difficult to cover the leaves uniformly with limestone, and easy to add too much, so that the resulting product contains more ground limestone than organic material.

❀ *Rotted Manure*

Some of the most beautiful plants we have ever grown indoors, as well as some of the worst, were planted in soil which had been mixed with rotted manure. Such extremes were discouraging—so discouraging, in fact, that we finally gave up using rotted manure in our soil mixtures entirely.

Out of doors, where plenty of space and sunshine prevail, where plants grow rapidly and rain leaches the soil, rotted manure carefully dug into our beds double-dyes our annuals with color and makes our vegetables grow twice as large in half the time.

Thanks to a long string of camp horses, we have plenty of source material. The compost piles in the orchard have been turned over two or three times each summer for four or five years, so that around the edges there are quantities of completely decomposed humus needing only to be picked up.

During the first two years of our experimental work, this well-decayed humus was used in a variety of combinations. We had mixed about 4 or 5 bushels of dirt with rotted manure, to be used as a foundation loam. The nitrogen content tested 35 parts per 1,000,000. To this, other materials were added in varying proportions. It often seemed like magic earth, for every soil mixture in which it was used produced good plants and, in some cases, exceptional ones. When our supply of soil containing rotted manure gave out, we went happily back to the orchard and gathered a new supply of humus from the identical pile that had contributed to our first foundation loam. As it was more completely rotted, we used a somewhat larger amount of soil. Naturally, we expected the same glorious results. Instead, we killed off our favorites—the begonia that always bloomed so gaily, but which we had not yet identified; the azalea we had nursed through the summer and fall, which was about to be forced into bloom; the maidenhair fern we had grown so proudly. Like others who lock the barn door after the horse is stolen, we quickly took the soil to the laboratory and analyzed it carefully. It contained 2500 parts of nitrogen per 1,000,000. Small wonder it had been a death-knell to our houseplants.

We carried on a long series of experiments, using dried cow, sheep, and horse manure, which could be extended as a basis for making a compost pile out of doors, for the indoor garden. However, it took from two to four years for these dried manures to decompose and leach sufficiently so that they could be incorporated into a soil mixture. The procedure was bothersome, and in the end meant time wasted. Rotted manure, we discovered, could be a fairy princess or a wolf in sheep's clothing. Seeking scientific results, we decided it could well be left alone. City-dwellers needed no substitute for country piles of rotted manure.

Careful soil analysis, of course, makes it possible to inculcate rotted manure into a soil. We have at hand superior equipment for soil analysis, but we now ignore our orchard compost piles when it comes to lamplight gardening. Actually, we have found there are much easier ways of feeding houseplants than by using so variable a material as a source of humus. So many scientific fertilizers have been developed that we can now pass by a barnyard without wishing to stop to ask the farmer for some manure.

FOOD FOR

YOUR PLANTS

From the days when an Indian planted a fish in the hole with his corn, it has been universally recognized that plants need added fertilization to grow well. Extensive research in the use of fertilizers has greatly broadened our horticultural knowledge. Nevertheless, most houseplants we have observed are put on a starvation diet. They go without breakfast, lunch, and dinner, while their owners wonder why they do not grow.

Just the same, it is better to half-starve your plants than to kill them with kindness. A plant will survive with too little fertilizer, but too much burns off the roots, causing the plant to die. Strive for the golden mean and err, if you must, on the side of too little fertilizer rather than too much.

No fertilizer is included in the soil recipes recommended here, because we found it was better to add it as needed rather than to incorporate it. Any plant potted in these soil mixtures should not be fertilized until the roots have grown through the soil to the edges of the pot. With most houseplants this usually occurs within two to four weeks from the time of potting, and with vegetable seedlings in a few days.

We have found that most houseplants under lights will be adequately fertilized if given nourishment at one-month intervals. Some that are growing very vigorously may need it every two weeks. Seedlings, however, must be fertilized frequently—usually once or twice a week.

Study your plants and learn to recognize which are rapid growers and which grow slowly. Naturally, you should fertilize the rapidly growing ones more often than you do the leisurely ones. A plant that stops growing in the middle of its growing cycle is usually in need of more fertilizer. A soil which becomes too acid will also stop plant growth, but if you have used our formula for the soil you can usually conclude that what it needs is additional nutriment.

Plants which are not getting enough nitrogen have a yellowish cast to their leaves, and the young leaves turn a clear yellow. We were surprised to have some cucumber leaves on a seedling only three weeks old become as yellow as a maple leaf in the fall. As soon as the seedling was given sufficient fertilizer, the leaves became a normal color. On the other hand, if the older leaves on a plant begin to turn yellow and die, it usually indicates that the roots have been injured by overfertilization.

Other factors, such as too much water, the lack of light, and unconsumed gas fumes, will also cause yellowing of the foliage. But if your plants are growing well generally, and yellow leaves appear on a few, you can safely conclude that they have had too much or too little fertilizer.

Of course, the only certain way to ascertain whether a soil is too rich or not is to test it. Simple tests for fertilizer elements have been devised by nearly every experimental station. By means of matching colors, one can determine quite accurately the nitrogen content of a soil, as well as the amounts of other elements present.

A water-soluble fertilizer containing nitrogen, phosphorus, and potassium in the ratio of 1–1–1 (it usually appears on the container label 20–20–20) is excellent to use for most houseplants. As you are dissolving it in water, make certain that it is not a fertilizer planned to be added to the soil but is a wettable powder. There are many commercial fertilizers on the market that are excellent, provided you read the label carefully.

Some plants need a fertilizer adapted to their particular needs, and special ones have been worked out for a number of plants. Azaleas do best with one with a proportion of 21–7–7. Before we knew anything about this, we watered a very beautiful azalea plant with an evenly balanced fertilizer only two times—and killed the plant. They are heavy nitrogen feeders, but cannot take too much phosphorus or potassium.

Lilies, too, like a different diet. A fertilizer has been developed for them with a ratio between the three substances of 16–4–12. The ratio for pot chrysanthemums is 15–10–30. If you are growing a number of these plants, it is worth making the effort to find the correct formula. Otherwise, use the all-purpose fertilizer, but sparingly.

Plants also need what are known as trace elements, such as iron, magnesium manganese, boron, sulfur, silicon, copper, zinc, and molybdenum. Most soils contain these elements, but if you are using Jiffy-Mix they must be added and it is a good safeguard with any soil. In making up our fertilizer solution, we also add a fertilizer containing these elements—that is, a soilless-culture mixture. It is desirable to use a fertilizer in which the source of nitrogen is urea rather than sodium nitrate. This is the recipe we use:

> *1 gallon of water*
> *1 level teaspoonful of a wettable powder or liquid 20–20–20 prepared fertilizer*
> *1 level teaspoonful of a soilless-culture mixture (Jiffy-Mix)*

Stir for at least two minutes to disolve all the soluble material. Sometimes a small portion remains as a residue. This is composed of inert, insoluble substances formed during the manufacture of the fertilizer; you can throw it away and feel that nothing is wasted. The soil should be moist when the fertilizer is applied. Do *not* fertilize your plants if you have forgotten to water them the preceding day.

If you are using automatic watering, the fertilizer should be applied from the top, after which the plants should be watered again to make certain that some of the fertilizer is washed down to the bottom of the pot.

The rule is to give the plants the same volume of fertilizer as of water in a single day.

THE ART OF WATERING

Fertilizing plants and watering them properly are closely interrelated. Plants obtain sufficient nourishment only when the soil is moist. This horticultural fact is often overlooked.

Many people refuse to believe that plants should be watered every day. They counter with the assertion "Overwatering kills your plants." This is true, but 99 per cent of all houseplants suffer from drought rather than from excess water.

There are two methods of watering plants; one entails the use of a sprinkling can, the other is automatic watering. If you have gone to all the trouble of mixing soil and installing lights, you will want to understand thoroughly the principles behind each system. You never can quite get away from a watering can, and yet for your tiny seedlings, vegetables, annuals, and perennials you will probably prefer to use automatic watering.

The philosophy of watering is well illustrated in terms of the out of doors. What gardeners call a "really good rain" does not just sprinkle the ground but saturates it thoroughly. It does not come down in a flood but falls gently for some time. Growing conditions are considered excellent when such a rain is followed by sunshine, so that the soil dries out gradually; but before it actually cakes and cracks, another good shower should come along. Try to give your plants these ideal conditions. A number of things will help.

The first important step is mental. Resolve to *water your plants every day*. Florists do, and, as you know, the atmosphere of the greenhouse is much more humid than that of the home. Sometimes it seems to us that the "green thumb" that good gardeners are supposed to possess may actually be summed up in this statement: they water their plants intelligently.

The second important step is to purchase a good watering can. A skillful waterer is able to use anything from a tumbler to a pitcher but a watering can with *a long spout* is a great help. Many types are on the market. One type has a spout two feet long, which makes it possible to reach all your plants easily. The tips of these spouts vary in diameter from ⅛ inch to ¼ inch. The smaller the opening, the smaller the stream they deliver. This is excellent for your plants, provided you do not skimp on the amount of water you give them. Sometimes it seems to take a long time to moisten the soil in a pot thoroughly with a small stream of water.

Our favorite watering device is a homemade gadget. It consists of a No. 10 can, to which a side-arm of ¼-inch copper tubing has been soldered ½ inch up the side from the bottom of the can. To this a 4-foot length of hose is attached; a second piece of copper tubing is bent at right angles to form the nozzle. The can works by gravity; it is hung high on a nail, or placed on top of the plant case. The hose is either pinched or bent and held against the nozzle to shut off the flow of water.

This homemade affair is unimpressive, but it is ideally adapted for use in a lamplight greenhouse. With it you can water plants in the back row of your four-by-six case very easily. If you are not equipped with a soldering iron, any tinsmith can fix the can for you at a nominal cost.

❀ How to Water

With your sprinkling device in hand and your thinking cap set firmly on your head, you are ready to water. Do not just draw the water from the tap, but test it as you do for a baby's bath by sticking your elbow in it. It must be just lukewarm—neither cold nor hot. Study, too, the needs of your plants. Our African violets, in three-inch pots, usually require about one-fourth of a cup of water apiece per day. The lucerna begonia, on the other hand, one of whose leaves is about equal to all the leaves of an African violet, takes at least four or five cups a day.

When the soil in a pot looks dry, pour on about ⅜ inch of water; if it looks quite wet, add ⅛ inch to ¼ inch. Add the water slowly. When a small amount seeps through the drainhole at the bottom, the plant is properly watered. If, in the course of a minute or two, no water has penetrated through, add more. Make a practice of letting only a small amount of water come through the hole, since large amounts of water will carry away the nutriments in the soil. But make sure it does come through; oftentimes you may need to add water two or three times if the soil is dried out. When you have learned to judge the needs of each plant more accurately, only a very small amount of water will seep through the drainhole. That is the whole story of correct watering.

But life is complex. Even in this simple operation there are a number of traps. You may have skipped a day or two so that the soil is thoroughly dried out and shrinks away from the sides of the pot, leaving a space around the edge. As you pour the water out of your sprinkling can, it will rush down the sides and come swiftly out the bottom, counterfeiting the real thing. If your thinking cap slips off, you can water your plants in this fashion and scarcely give them a drop to drink, as the ball of earth is completely dried out and the water will not penetrate.

When the soil in a pot is dried out, it must be thoroughly soaked, pot and all. Submerge the pot in a pan of water so that the water comes nearly to the rim. Remove the pot as soon as the soil is moist. With your fingers press the soil back against the sides of the pot so the gap will be closed and you can water normally again.

You can achieve the same result—but it takes more care—by watering the plant from the top and pressing the soil firmly against the sides with the fingers. The soil, as it gets wet, swells. The process will have to be repeated three or four times before the soil is thoroughly moist. The first method is usually safer for a beginner.

Sometimes the drain opening in the bottom of a flowerpot will become sealed off. This prevents the water from draining through, and the soil becomes waterlogged. You can detect that a pot is not draining when water remains for some time on the surface of the soil. Correct the difficulty immediately, for plants cannot live long in water. Drainholes occasionally become sealed off when pots rest on a very smooth surface. Usually there is sufficient dirt or unevenness on a bench to prevent this from happening; but if you have trouble with it, the pots may be set on a hardware cloth, pebbles, or a layer of vermiculite.

You can tell whether soil is too wet or too dry by touching the surface with your finger. Dry soil is firm, and very little will adhere to your finger. Moist soil is soft, and much more will adhere, leaving your finger somewhat soiled. Watersoaked soil is so wet that the water will ooze out when you press it. This usually occurs only when your flowerpot is placed within a decorative container. Should this happen, immediately empty the water from the jardiniere and take pot and plant to the kitchen sink. Lay the pot on its side, and the excess water which has collected in the soil will drain off. It is probably best to leave the plant on its side for about a half-hour, because the roots of the plant will die if they are allowed to remain in watersoaked soil. After draining off the water from a watersoaked plant, do not water it until the surface of the soil again has a normal appearance. Soil is always darker when wet; as you observe its color, you will gain experience in gauging the amounts of water needed.

When all is said and done, watering from the top is an *art*, and many fail to learn it. However, there are other ways of watering plants. Self-watering devices are not difficult to install, and the plants thrive with this method of watering.

❀ Automatic Watering

We were slow to investigate automatic watering because we ourselves had mastered the art of watering, but once we had used it we became enthusiastic devotees of the system and installed it wherever we could. Unlike many automatic devices, an automatic watering system is not difficult to provide and entails very little expense. Because it keeps the soil constantly moist, the plants grow much better, and the system saves you hours of time.

One of the simplest forms is the wick method. It is possible to purchase special flowerpots that are designed to be used with a wick, but it is an easy matter to adapt any container. Just as a lamp wick carries oil to the flame, such a wick carries water into the soil as the plant absorbs it.

Wicks may be made of asbestos rope, cylindrical fiberglass manufactured for the purpose, or pieces of cotton cloth or burlap made into a ¼-inch cylindrical roll and held in place with string. About 1½ inches of one end of the wick are frayed and unraveled and spread out in the bottom of the pot. The other end is threaded through the drainhole and rests in water. The pot is rested on a support to keep it above the water. Empty tunafish cans, well washed, with a hole punched in the center of the bottom for the wick to pass through, make excellent stands for pots in jardinieres.

Your plants will grow much better as soon as you adopt this method, for it ensures a constant water supply. Of course, you need to keep the water replenished. Washing and packing of the soil is also eliminated.

Seedlings which are being grown in flats can be watered with wicks too. Holes about four inches apart each way are drilled through the bottom of the flat, and wicks run through the holes into a pan underneath, which is filled with water. Watch the flat to make sure it does not dry out even slightly, but generally it will not if the reservoir below is kept supplied with water.

In your indoor greenhouse you will find it time-saving, easier, and very effective to use a pan equipped with a pipe for watering. Any tinsmith can make up the pans for you, using galvanized iron. Some authorities recommend that these galvanized pans should be carefully painted first with asphaltum so as to avoid any chance of zinc poisoning of the plants. We prefer small pans to the larger ones because they are easier to put into and take out of the greenhouse, and much easier to keep level, an important factor in the success of the system. We use PVC plastic pipe, which is easily available and easy to work with, in pans 10 by 20 inches or 14 by 24 inches. Avoid using copper pipe, as it too can poison your plants. The pipe is placed in the pan as close to its center as possible. Make certain that the pan is level; you will have no trouble if you have built your greenhouse with a level base. If your pan is on a bench or a table, you may need to prop up one side or the other. Drill holes along one side of the pipe at 2-inch intervals. Bend it into an L-shape, squeeze one end shut, and seal it. Bend the other end upward and pour the water through. After the pipe is installed, block off a corner of the pan (one you can see easily) with a piece of glass or sheet metal 4 to 6 inches long, and as high as the sides of the pan. This makes a triangular opening, with the piece of glass as the base and the corner as the apex. The rest of the pan is filled with insulation-grade vermiculite to a depth of 2 inches. By means of your triangular peep-hole you can ascertain the depth of the water.

Add the water by pouring it into the nipple with a watering can or other container, and with the help of a funnel if necessary. The first time, a 14-by-24-inch pan may take a gallon or more of water to wet the vermiculite. Add water till you have a depth of 1¼ to 1½ inches in the triangle-shaped well you have made. If you happen to have more than 2 inches of vermiculite, the water level will need to be somewhat higher. It should be kept ¾ inch below the surface. Vermiculite does not float on the water; water penetrates it.

Of course, sand or gravel could be used in this system in place of vermiculite, but both sand and gravel are so heavy, together with the water, that a very firm support must be made to hold the pans.

Once the pans are prepared, all that you need to do is to place the pots on the vermiculite, and they will automatically absorb the water. While in some instances we have not had to add water for a week, with a large number of pots in one pan you will probably need to add water every day. It is preferable to have the pots well watered before placing them in the pans. You must be cautious about the amount of water you use. If you use too much, the pots will sink into the vermiculite and may topple over.

When it is time to fertilize the plants that are being automatically watered, we water each pot separately with a watering can. A fairly safe rule is to add 1 cubic inch of the fertilizer solution to each 6 or 8 cubic inches of soil. Thus, a 3-inch flowerpot requires 3 tablespoons of the fertilizer solution. A 4-inch pot requires ⅓ cup of solution; a 5-inch pot, ½ cup; a 6-inch pot, ¾ cup.

If you are using automatic watering for seedlings that you plan to transplant out of doors, and they are in bands, it is very easy to figure the number of cubic inches of soil, and to add the proper amount of fertilizer solution each week. Fertilize when the depth of water is low.

Installing automatic watering does not relieve you of the necessity of keeping a watchful eye on your plants to see that they do not dry out. Oftentimes it will be necessary to water some from the top. Cucumber, melon, squash, and lettuce seedlings use a great deal of water and will probably need additional amounts.

POTS AND

TRANSPLANTING

Plants may be hardy, but they respond better to coddling than to being asked to show their Spartan qualities. Oftentimes mistaken kindness forces them to grow under conditions that are not to their liking. One of the most familiar misconceptions concerns the size of the flowerpot.

We used to discard the small-sized pot as soon as we purchased a newly rooted cutting. We wanted to give it a chance to grow and felt that a 5-inch pot would make it understand that it had found a true friend. Usually the little plant failed to respond, since so much soil and so little light gave it a new set of problems.

A well-lighted greenhouse is a great help. The large-sized pot is not always such a disaster, because the roots grow fast enough to fill the bigger pot. Yet now the great majority of our plants are in 3-inch pots, only a few in the 4-, 5-, and 6-inch sizes. It is far better to begin with the small pots, and to transplant to the larger ones as the plant and its roots increase in size.

Most indoor gardeners need to use the large-sized pots because they water their plants so sparingly. Usually, the small pots do necessitate daily watering, but plants give their thanks for this understanding of their actual needs by producing flowers.

Just as a craftsman fits the shoe to his last, you must fit the size of the pots to your plants. You would never think of recommending that everyone wear size 10 shoes, so it is impossible to generalize on just how large a pot should be used for each plant. If you visit a professional greenhouse, you will notice that most of the plants are being grown in a 2¼- or 2½-inch pot. This is not to conserve space, as many people falsely assume, but to give the plants a chance to grow well.

You will give the same boost to your plants by putting them in pots that fit their root systems. To determine what sizes you need, tip plants out of their pots and examine the root systems.

Getting a plant out of its pot and into another is something of a job for a beginner. Watching an expert move, or, as he would probably say, "shift" a plant from a small-sized pot to a larger one, you would think there was nothing to it. He holds the pot in one hand, steadying the plant by keeping the stem between his fingers. Then he turns it upside down, gives the rim a sharp knock against the bench, and plant and dirt come gracefully out of the pot in a single compact mass. He deftly fluffs out the roots if they are matted together, drops a little dirt into his new pot, slips the plant into it, places some dirt around the edges and firmly presses it down with his thumbs. The operation takes less than a minute, and at the end the plant looks as though it had lived in the new pot all its life.

But, like many things, from dancing to serving a tennis ball, it is not as easy as it looks. Nine times out of ten, when you tap the rim hopefully against the table, nothing happens; or you break off several leaves; or just some of the dirt comes out. Rarely do plant and dirt slip out together.

There is a small trick, however, which will make the job easier for you. When you transfer a plant, put a piece of broken pot over the drainhole at the bottom of the new container. Use a piece that is two or three times larger than the hole it covers. Then, when you wish to examine the roots of the plant or move it to larger quarters, all you have to do is push a pencil through the bottom hole, press it firmly against the piece of broken pot, and plant and dirt will slip out of the pot, just as they do for an expert.

The broken piece of pot has another function, which is more important for the plant. It prevents the dirt from being washed through the drainhole. So, even if you are deft at repotting, do not give up the crockery.

If the grower has not used this method, and you cannot dislodge the root system, it may be necessary to break the pot to remove the plant; crack it by hitting it with a small hammer or a screwdriver. This method means beginning again with a new pot, but this business of the right pot for the right plant is important. You can afford to sacrifice pots, but you cannot afford to damage the root system by pulling or yanking on the plant. It is not serious if the ball of earth fails to come out in one piece, provided the rootlets are not broken off. After the first few tries, you will have considerably less trouble.

Study very carefully the way the roots are growing. Their appearance will tell you whether the plant should go into a smaller pot, into a larger one, or back into the same pot. A plant whose roots are hidden in the ball of earth has been overpotted. When the soil is well penetrated by the roots, and firm white rootlets stretch far down the sides of the pot, the time is ripe for a larger pot. In the soil recommended here, roots grow from the center straight out to the sides of the pot, so that all the soil is honeycombed with fine root hairs.

In some soils you will find that the roots stretch near the surface and partly down the sides, and that there are very few in the ball of earth. This is a plant's way of saying it *does not like* the soil. Wash the soil off the roots, and give it soil that will be more to its liking.

Sometimes the roots are tangled and entwined round and round the sides of the pot. In this case you have waited too long before giving the plant a bigger home, so you must gently pull the matted roots apart. They should stretch out around the ball of earth like a full skirt. In this position they will get the most benefit from the new soil. Sift the new soil in around the roots, so that as few as possible will be forced together again. Usually you can separate them enough so that a normal root system will develop. Add enough soil so that it comes up to the rim of the pot; then firm it down with the tips of your fingers. The soil should be somewhat moist, but not wet. At first you may be a little nervous and clumsy-fingered, but with experience you will find it a simple matter to turn a plant out of its pot or to transplant it, as the case may be. It is an art you must learn, because looking at a plant's roots tells you more about its needs than anything else does.

When you find that a plant needs transplanting, shift it to a pot of the next larger size. Flowerpots are made in standard sizes which are listed according to their diameters. There are also pots not as tall as the standard size, known as the three-quarters, and others, half as tall, which are referred to as "pans." The three-quarter pots prove very handy for azaleas, dracaenas, and other plants with large root systems which quickly outgrow small pots. Bulbs are usually planted in pans. These will also, as a rule, just fit the root system of a begonia or a fern.

A few plants must be adjusted to pots not because of the size of their roots but because of the size of their thirst. Some geraniums, the lucerna begonia, and other plants would require watering twice a day if their pots were selected to correspond to the size of their root systems. They must be given good-sized pots to survive.

All plants should be watered as soon as they are transplanted. The best system is to plunge the newly potted plant in a pan of water, with the water up to the rim of the flowerpot; leave it there until the soil is moist, Clean, dry pots are great consumers of moisture, so unless a plant is treated in this manner, there is danger that the porous-textured surface of the pot will suck all the water from the soil, leaving it dry.

❀ Clean Pots

Clean, well-sterilized flowerpots are almost as important to plants as are pots of the right size; it is imperative to have them clean before they are used. Few gardeners realize how important it is to have pots that always look new, even though appearance is not the most important aspect involved.

All that is necessary is to put the used pots in a pail of water and leave them there to soak for several days; then pour off the soiled water and refill the pail with clean water. An additional three-day soaking will dissolve practically anything that still adheres. Remove the pots from the water and wipe off the film that covers them. If some are still soiled, do not scrub them; just return them to the pail and soak them till they can be easily cleaned.

When you have a dozen or so pots, stack them in a pan and sterilize them in the oven at 300 degrees Fahrenheit for two hours. They will look as though they had just come from the potter's kiln. You can use them with the assurance that neither pests nor spores of algae adhere to them.

MEET THE ENEMY

AND ATTACK

The utmost precautions must be taken to keep your indoor green-house and your collection of plants free from pests. Clean pots are but one link in the chain that must be forged with vigilance; for growing plants under artificial lights does not create a Garden of Eden, with neither hidden mites to gnaw on the blossoms nor tiny bugs in the soil to sap the strength of the plants. Like the goblins, they come in "if you don't watch out."

It is far easier to keep them out than to get them out. Quite often these uninvited guests arrive on a blossoming plant. Rightly or wrongly, you will soon learn to become suspicious of any new arrival; this is a healthy attitude. You can save yourself considerable trouble by establishing a port of entry, a sort of Ellis Island, where all new plants are kept and observed. Some may have to stay in quarantine for an indefinite period; others can be given a "safety first" treatment and then released. Occasionally you may have to throw away a new plant to avoid the risk of contaminating the others.

Large numbers of soil pests are eliminated when you sterilize the soil. This is the most effective extended coverage possible in lamplight gardening. Numerous creatures, so tiny that you cannot see them, lurk in the soil. Viewing them through the microscope makes you feel glad that you cannot see them all the time. A small white grub, not more than ¼ inch in length, has jaws half its size with which it chews the plants. Another is redheaded and somewhat larger. In addition, there are soil aphids, garden centipedes, wireworms, slugs, and small white worms sometimes called "wigglers." All told, they are a sorry lot that does much damage to the root system of your plants.

Many plants you buy are potted in an unsterilized soil mixture. We meet this menace in a manner that would make a professional grower's hair stand on end; before a plant is placed in our greenhouse, we wash the old soil away from the roots and replace it with a properly sterilized soil mixture. Although the practice is unorthodox, it pays 100-per-cent dividends; you can keep out the enemy, give your plant a good soil, and have the opportunity to examine the roots when they are bare of earth. The worst soil pest of all, the nematode, may be hidden there. Examine the roots under a magnifying glass to see whether they are swollen and kinked. If you see these bad signs, sigh sadly (or curse softly) and quickly throw out dirt, plant, and water. Fortunately, you will not find the nematode often.

Of the many pests that live above the ground, one is the bane of African-violet growers—the cyclamen mite. We met it on the first batch of African violets we purchased. It proved to be a blessing in disguise, for our research on how to eliminate it along with the other mites (without also eliminating the plants) went hand-in-hand with our work on soils and the growing of plants under artificial lights.

Of course, we never suspected that the cyclamen mite was the enemy in our midst on those first African violets, and you will probably never suspect, either, that it is present. It is hard to visualize how small these mites really are. It would take several hundred placed end to end to stretch out an inch. You can't see them with the naked eye, and they are hard for most people to locate even with a microscope. Viewed under a lens, they appear as pale brown, translucent, oval specks, with thick legs and heads out of all proportion to the rest of their bodies. You really can discover their presence only by recognizing the damage they do. If the new growth of leaves or flowers seems wrinkled, pale in color, or deformed, you should immediately become suspicious. A very detailed description of the calling cards left by the cyclamen mites is given in the chapter on African Violets (Chapter 28), because these are the plants you must particularly watch, although other plants invaded by these mites are treated just as badly.

Most pests seem to have close relatives. New ones that you have never seen before are always popping up. Few people can recognize the specific individual, but it is not difficult to become acquainted with some representatives in the general classifications. Sometimes, as you study the insects that prey on plants in your lamplight greenhouse, you wonder that there are any plants at all.

In the days when we were studying pests, we gave a green-leafed fatsia a special welcome, not because of the rather unattractive large-leafed plant, but because both the two-spotted spider mite and the red spider mite lurked on it.

We had a brood area for pests. It was a dreary-looking place under a two-tubed fluorescent fixture. Each plant stood alone in solitary splendor, mounted on stilts and surrounded by water. Here the green-leafed fatsia was given a special place of honor. For several months we pursued our investigation; would certain insecticides kill off the pests or the plant first? The fatsia proved hardy, and after all kinds of experimental treatment lived in pest-free glory to a ripe old age.

The two-spotted spider mite gets its name from the black spots on its body. It is somewhat larger than some of the red spider mites, and varies in color from a pale yellowish-green to a light green.

Practically the entire body of the red spider mite is red, varying in shade from pinkish to deep red. The red spider mite is gregarious, lives in colonies, and multiplies very fast. These pests feed first on the bottom side of the leaf, and as this becomes overpopulated some of them move upstairs, while their brothers pick other ports of migration.

It is high time to investigate a plant when you notice a leaf turning yellow. There are many other things besides the spider mite which cause yellowing leaves; however, a leaf upon which the mites are feeding becomes, first, a lighter green, then fades to yellow, and sometimes becomes bronzy, owing to the presence of the insects, which by this time number literally in the thousands.

To a large extent, unless you continually use a high-power magnifying glass, these minute insects have to be identified by the effects they produce. As you train yourself to watch the appearance of the leaves on your plants, you will be able to recognize more quickly the presence of mites.

Any number of other troublesome pests can be quite easily distinguished without a glass. Among these are three large and prevalent types: the mealy bug, scale, and aphids.

The mealy bug is encased in what looks like a frothy white marshmallow coating that seems to be full of air bubbles.

There are many different kinds of scale. The most common are the soft brown scale and the ivy scale. The name "soft brown scale" is misleading, for invariably, when you first see it, the scale is a hard brown lump about ⅛ inch in diameter. The ivy scale is a deep brown, but against the green of the leaves appears almost black. It is considerably smaller than the soft brown scale.

Aphids seem to appear without reason on one's plants. Under a magnifying glass they look something like grasshoppers, with large abdomens and long legs. They have long, pointed snouts, with which they stab through the leaf tissue and suck the juices. There are numerous kinds of these pests, too.

Rush to the attack as soon as you discover signs of any pest, and continue the assault until you come out victorious. The warfare with pests is much more of a life-and-death struggle than you may realize. Either you get the pests, or the pests will get your plants.

The crusade is made much more difficult because you are operating in a home instead of in an outdoor greenhouse. Many sprays and insecticides which are the stock-in-trade of commercial growers are ruled out, for in your home they would poison not only the pests but the inhabitants. Other methods, such as systemic poisoning, are not advised either. In a large greenhouse, plants grow so well and so rapidly that it is not toxic to them; in the home, unless your light intensity is high, it is.

A certain and easy way of getting rid of the three worst pests, the cyclamen mite, the spider mite, and the mealy bug, is to throw out the plants. We shall never forget our son's amazement when, one day, he took the cover off our largest garbage can, and found it filled to the brim with African violets. We had just finished throwing out about one hundred twenty-five plants that showed signs of harboring the cyclamen mite.

We maintained that it was quicker and safer to grow new plants from well-treated leaves than to take chances on these older plants. Our son thought one of us must have gone suddenly mad, but we explained, "Clean plants blossom so profusely, it's well worth the sacrifice." Moreover, plants grow so rapidly under artificial lights that replacing suspected plants with healthy ones is not the problem it would be under windowsill conditions.

Today, although we have found ways of using insecticides that kill the pests but do not affect the plants, we still resort, at times, to our original method of throwing out a plant that harbors a cyclamen mite. It is a time-honored practice that we recommend.

Very effective sprays and dips were discarded because they failed to pass the safety standards we had for home use. Everything considered, we finally settled for Malathion in a 25-per-cent wettable powder. It is excellent as a spray or a dip to get rid of such unpleasant pests as aphids, leafminers, mealy bug, white flies, scales, and lace bugs. Five tablespoonfuls are mixed in a gallon of water.

We were greatly helped in our search for *safe* insecticides by the research which has been done at Cornell University. Their pamphlet *A Guide to Safe Pest Control around the Home*, Bulletin 74, gives a number of controls. For mites Cornell recommends the use of Dicofol (Kelthane) which is an 18.5-per-cent wettable powder, and is used 2 tablespoonfuls to 1 gallon of water. For mildew fungi mix 2 teaspoonfuls of dinocap (Karathane) in 1 gallon of water. Boston and English ivies are given to a leafspot disease which can be treated with copper fungicide used as either a spray or a dip. With these insecticides, you can face pests without panic.

You will always find it more effective to dip a plant than to spray it. Insects persist on the undersides of leaves, in crevices, and on new growth. Dipping completely coats the plant and gets at the insects hidden in the crevices.

The mealy bug, which seems to accept any plant as fair game, is usually routed by thoroughly washing the plant with rubbing alcohol. This treatment does not affect the plant if it is well rinsed after being washed. It is necessary to wash the pot as well as the plant with alcohol, and sometimes you will need to give a second treatment.

Nicotine sulfate in a water solution with Vel detergent is also effective in getting rid of scale. To make the dipping solution, take 1 quart of lukewarm water and add ½ teaspoonful of Vel. Stir so that the water is frothy and bubbly. Because research has proved any form of nicotine poisonous, be sure, when you use it, to wear gloves and keep the solution away from your skin. Ivies, holly, or any plant covered with scale can be dipped in this solution, and the pests will float away.

In dipping a plant, the pot is held in one hand while the other is used to hold the ball of earth so it doesn't fall out when the plant is upside-down. We usually use a mop pail. If you have a plant that is too large to dip, it is possible to spray it. In that case, it is best to wear a respirator, or to place a moist towel over your nose and mouth. An hour or two after the spraying, the plant should be washed gently but thoroughly in a stream of lukewarm water.

It is unlikely that your seedlings will have any pests on them, but be on the watch. Pests have a strange way of suddenly putting in an appearance. If you discover any, use the same insecticide and the same methods on your seedlings that you use on the ornamental plants you are growing under lights. *All* plants should be thoroughly washed with clear water an hour or two after being treated with insecticide. If you do this, no injury to them will ever result.

Pests are troublesome, but with these sprays and with constant watchfulness you can control them.

SEED-SOWING

Seed-planting may be a ritual, a breathtaking promise, or a job attended with misgivings. Many of us have had the disappointing experience of planning to grow our annuals and vegetables, only to have the seeds fail to germinate, damp off, or produce such spindly plants that we decide it is better, after all, to buy them. The use of artificial lights changes all this and adds the longed-for spice of certainty to the task of growing seedlings.

Great advances have been made in germinating seeds through the discovery that many varieties of seeds are light sensitive—that is, they germinate only in the light, and poorly or not at all when covered with soil. This knowledge has made it possible to germinate many ornamental plants by starting them under lights.

We grew seeds under lights for years without understanding this principle. The system we developed was hardly orthodox, but it worked, and we came to feel it was practically foolproof. Looking at it today, in the light of the work that has been done by plant scientists, we can see that we actually gave some of the seeds more light than they needed. We are explaining the system here in detail because it is so easy for the amateur to use. The directions, however, must be followed to the smallest detail. Change it only for the special seeds that need to be grown in the dark. (See Appendix II.)

Each step of our system has been carefully checked by numerous experiments with many different types of seeds. We judged its effectiveness by the fact that with "good seeds" the percentage of germination recorded on the package was nearly equaled in the seeds that sprouted. Our error was in not knowing that some of the poor seeds might have been turned into "good seeds" had they been given complete darkness—but the number was very small.

For light we use two incandescent 40-watt bulbs with only an ordinary shade* two feet away from the seedbed. It is important to store the seeds you buy carefully. Do not leave them around; store them in your refrigerator at 40 degrees Fahrenheit until you are ready to use them. The important essential is never to let the seeds dry out. They will be a total loss if they dry out for only a few hours.

To eliminate this danger completely, we plant all of our seeds in standard 4-inch pans, which we set in pans of water 1½ inches deep. Since the tiny seedlings are transplanted as soon as they can be handled, this procedure does not cause the roots of the seeds to decay from lack of oxygen or excess moisture. The seed pots must be completely clean and sterilized, both the 4-inch pans in which they are germinated and the smaller ones into which they are transplanted. Just as you see that everything connected with your newborn baby is sterilized, be equally careful with your seed babies. Sterilize everything you use; although a new, clean pot is probably safe, take no chances. To prepare the pot for sowing the seeds, place a piece of sheet metal over the opening in the bottom. You can use a disk cut from a tin can with tinner's snips, or, if you don't have any such snips, you can use a pair of heavy household shears (this is an act of desperation, for it dulls the shears). A copper coin will not do; neither will a quarter. A piece of broken pot will not work, for the vermiculite that is used as a planting medium is likely to wash through the hole. A firmer seedbed can be made if you have available both the insulating grade of vermic-

---

* We have also used one 60-watt bulb successfully and some people have been able to germinate some kinds of seeds with as little as ½ foot-candle of light.

ulite and the really coarse perlite sometimes called Horticulture Grade.

Cover the bottom of the pot with a handful or two of the coarse perlite; then add the finer well-screened vermiculite. Fill the pot to within ¾ inch from the top. As a safety precaution, we wet the vermiculite by pouring boiling water into the pot until it comes out the hole in the bottom. This is practically akin to sterilizing the vermiculite. As it is an inert substance, this precaution is probably unnecessary, but we pay double respect to cleanliness when it comes to germinating seeds. Should you wish to use the pot immediately, it may be cooled by running cold water through the vermiculite.

Several different kinds of seeds may be planted in one pot. A 4-inch pan will hold well over three hundred seeds, for at this stage of their development seedlings do not need elbow room. We plant the seeds in rows about ½ inch apart, separating the different varieties with toothpick markers. Generally you will have no trouble in distinguishing one type of seedling from another. A whole row or two of lettuce or onions will come up in a rush. There are always a few stragglers, but not many—so it is a simple matter to recognize the different varieties even when they are only tiny specks.

To make doubly sure that the seeds remain moist, each pot is covered with a piece of plate glass. The pot is then placed in a baking pan containing 1½ inches of water. As the water evaporates or is absorbed by the pot, it must be replenished. Usually a little water must be added each day.

We germinate our seeds in the basement, where the temperature is always quite warm and fairly constant. It ranges, day and night, between 72 and 78 degrees Fahrenheit. All kinds of seeds have germinated for us at this temperature. We had nearly 100-per-cent germination of delphinium seeds even though delphiniums are supposed to prefer a temperature of 55 degrees to do their best. There was considerable variation in the germination time. About half of them came up in six days; the stragglers took another two weeks.

Seed germination by this method is so certain that it offers the amateur an excellent means of testing the seeds he wishes to plant either indoors or out of doors.

Seedlings, whether they are ornamentals, vegetables, or flowers, should be transplanted from the seed pan into soil *as soon as they can be handled.* With the aid of a spatula or a thin-bladed knife, it is possible to lift practically any seedlings twenty-four hours after the first show of life appears above the surface of the vermiculite. The spatula or knife is used as though it were a tiny spade; stick it in beside the row of seedlings that has appeared, and push upward to loosen the vermiculite. Most vegetable seedlings can then be gently held between the thumb and forefinger and transplanted into soil. Flower annuals, however, usually come from such very small seed that the only way they can be moved is to rest them lightly on the knife or the spatula.

The system has many advantages. To us the most spectacular is that we have never had any trouble with damping off. By transplanting into sterilized soil as soon as possible after the seeds germinate, we have never lost a seedling for this reason. If the system is to work, there must be no delay in transplanting; be sure to have everything ready before you plant a single seed—pots, soil, and greenhouse.

If the seedlings are left in the vermiculite until the cotyledons begin to open, the stems will be elongated an inch or two, depending on the light intensity. If the seedlings are transplanted almost immediately (within twenty-four hours) after germination, the cotyledons will have grown about three-eighths of an inch above the ground and the resulting plants will be stockier. As soon as the transplanting has been completed, the seedlings can take full advantage of our indoor greenhouse. There they will have a high light intensity, a high temperature, a long day, and can also be treated with carbon dioxide, which greatly stimulates the growth of leaf and tissue of young seedlings.

Two groups of tomato plants illustrated for us the importance of transplanting as soon as the seedlings could be handled. One group was transplanted into pots a day after the seeds germinated, the second group six days after germinating, when the cotyledons had opened. Aside from this difference of six days, both sets of seedlings were grown under identical conditions of light and temperature: a light intensity of 1500 foot-candles, a 16-hour day, and a temperature between 65 and 70 degrees Fahrenheit. Those that had been transplanted early continued to hold their advantage, and six weeks later, when they were ready to be set out in the garden, they were definitely superior plants.

Many a vegetable seedling with only ¼ inch of top growth boasts a

1- or 1½-inch rootlet. This elementary root is known technically as a radicle. In soil it develops rapidly. One of our asparagus seedlings, for example, had an above-ground growth of ¼ inch, and a radicle 4½ inches long. It was transplanted two and a half days after the seed germinated, and was fertilized with the regular fertilizing solution four days later. At this time the tiny root hairs were pushing through the soil in all directions. Of course, the asparagus is famous for its roots, but it is not exceptional to have other vegetable seedlings grow with as much vigor, even though they have radicles only ¼ inch long when they are shifted into soil.

Transplanting twenty-four hours after germination also saves root injury and much time. If the roots are allowed to grow in the vermiculite, and especially if they are fed with some fertilizer before being transplanted, they grow long and tangle together. One needs to be deft and patient to extricate the different plantlets, and some roots are certain to be broken. When you use the quick-transplanting method, the seedlings come out of the vermiculite easily; they are clean, too, for the vermiculite shakes off easily.

The fact that the roots grow so rapidly, however, poses a problem for lamplight gardeners. If the seedlings become potbound, their growth will be stunted, so that you will lose many of the benefits of having started them early. On the other hand, as space under lights is somewhat limited, it is a temptation to use a container that is too small.

Seedlings may be transplanted into flats, pots, or bands. Pots are the best. Every time a seedling is transplanted it receives a setback, so if you can eliminate one transplanting, you will have earlier vegetables and flowers.

Don't hesitate to place the tiny speck of a seedling in a 2½-inch pot. It will fill the container quickly. In any case, do not use wooden bands smaller than 2 by 2 inches, or pots smaller than 2¼ inches. If you use a flat, space the seedlings 2½ inches apart.

Remember, the primary essential is that pots and bands be absolutely clean and that the soil be sterilized. We repeat this here because of its great importance.

To transplant seedlings, first make a hole with a nail or a pointed stick. The seedling should be placed in the hole in such a manner that, if possible, the rootlet does not touch the sides. Rootlets are very tender and break easily. After the seedling has been placed in the hole, the dirt is firmed around it, and it is well watered. The pot or band is placed under lights in a pan equipped with automatic watering. Except for fertilizing it, you can just stand back and watch it grow. If you use bands, the seed flat needs to be deep enough to allow space for 1 inch of vermiculite under them, plus the height of the band.

We prefer to use flowerpots. We find them more economical because they can be cleaned and sterilized and used over and over again, while paper or wooden bands can be used twice at the most, and they are much harder to clean and sterilize. Clay pots have a practical advantage, too. Because of their slanting sides, and the practice of putting a piece of crockery over the drainhole, you can remove plants from these without disturbing the roots more easily than you can from any other type of container.

It is difficult to grow good seedlings unless you use automatic watering of some sort from the start. Few of us can keep seedlings constantly wet enough to ensure good growth by using a watering can. Automatic watering ensures success. It is best to use either the pipe in a pan filled with vermiculite or the wick method described in Chapter 19.

Lettuce, beets, peas, and other cold-weather crops can be given a fine start under your fluorescent lights, and then be transplanted immediately to the garden, thus making room for the more tender vegetables that must be grown under lights until all danger of frost is over.

Seedlings grow so rapidly that they must be fertilized frequently. Usually it is not necessary to fertilize them until the fourth day after they have been transplanted; some will not need fertilizer for seven days. Fast growers such as melons, squash, and cucumbers must be fertilized more often than once a week.

❀ Testing Your Seeds

Testing the response of seeds to light is one of the many scientific advances that growing plants under lights has made possible. Seed-testing is a wide-open field, not only for young scientists but for gardeners as well. You will enjoy knowing how it is done.

The discovery that some seeds will not germinate in darkness has had a revolutionary effect on both agriculture and horticulture. For generations most new-sown seeds have been sprinkled—lightly—with soil. Sprinkling lightly may have been the saving grace, enabling light-hungry seeds to see the light. The light needs of seeds differ widely. One short exposure may be enough for some seeds, while others may need light for four or five days. Other seeds will germinate only in darkness. Gardeners have inadvertently given preference to dark-loving seeds for years.

Actually, there are many seeds which are fairly tolerant of the environment during the germination process, and others which have quite precise requirements. Thanks to the careful research that has been done by Henry M. Cathey of the Crops Research Department of the United States Department of Agriculture, the indoor gardener does not need to wonder about the germination of his garden seeds, or ornamental herb seeds, or plants he wishes to grow in pots. These have been tested, and their requirements are listed. (See Appendix III.)

In the experiments that were carried out, seeds were tested by being kept in darkness while they germinated. Others were exposed to 300 foot-candles of coolwhite fluorescent light. Regardless of their special requirements, most of the seeds germinated when they were given light, a moist atmosphere, and a fairly constant warm temperature. These are the basic requirements of our method of seed germination.

If you are interested in testing your seeds for the effects of light and temperature, you can use the same method that has been designed for science students. To carry out the following experiment, you need only two 40-watt fluorescent coolwhite tubes.

You will also need four plastic-covered dishes marked 1 through 4. Plastic sandwich boxes with lids are very good, or you can buy Petri dishes at a chemical supply store. In addition, you should have sheets of blue and red cellophane, blotters or paper toweling, and aluminum foil so that the dishes can be wrapped to provide total darkness.

In many experiments, the seeds are prepared for planting in the same way. Cut several layers of paper toweling or blotters to fit into the bottom of each dish. Next, soak the paper thoroughly and be sure it is completely saturated. The excess water is then poured off.

Now sprinkle the seeds over the paper. If you have plenty of seeds, one hundred makes a good number in each dish because it is easier to figure percentages, although ten in a dish is sufficient. As soon as the seeds are sown, close the covers and wrap all the dishes in aluminum foil. Use two layers of foil so you are certain they are in total darkness. After the seeds have been moisture-soaked in darkness for 16 to 24 hours, they are ready for the experiments.

Boxes 1 and 2 are kept at the same temperature, 70 degrees Fahrenheit, for the period of the experiment. Boxes 3 and 4 are kept in changing temperatures: 60 degrees for the first day and 77 degrees thereafter.

Boxes 1 and 3 are kept in darkness throughout the period. Boxes 2 and 4 are exposed to light in the following manner: remove the aluminum foil once a day and expose the boxes to light from the fluorescent tubes for 1 hour; then, return them to darkness by carefully rewrapping them in aluminum foil. As soon as the seeds in some of the boxes germinate, the experiment is complete. Open all the boxes and count the seeds that have germinated. If the seeds in boxes 2 and 4 have sprouted, you will know that your seeds are light-sensitive. You can measure the relative effects of temperature on the seeds by comparing the boxes containing the germinated seeds to see which appear to be more advanced in their development.

STARTING YOUR GARDEN FLOWERS

A number of the favorite annuals require long exposures to light to germinate, and this is a fact worth remembering. The much-loved petunia is a very light-conscious seed. Others in the same class are aster, bachelor's button, coreopsis, forget-me-not, phlox, rudbeckia, scabiosa, snapdragon, and verbena. Give the seeds an 18-hour day. Some will surprise you by showing their first cotyledon in a day or two. As soon as you have planted them in soil, shortly after they have germinated, shorten the day to 10 hours. The short day will inhibit flowering, but it stimulates the leaf and stem growth so that in six or eight weeks you will have the stockiest, bushiest annuals you have ever had, plants that will reward you with flowers the summer through.

Be sure you have an illumination of at least 1000 foot-candles. More light is better. It is not hard to obtain because the small seedlings can be moved quite close to the lamps.

The real danger is that, forgetting how well seedlings grow indoors under artificial lights, you will follow your former planting schedule. There is nothing more discouraging than having big, healthy plants languish under too little light in the house when it is too cold to set them out.

For example, the so-called French marigold, which differs in its light requirements from the regular garden marigold, is a long-day plant and, under a light intensity of from 600 to 750 foot-candles for 18 hours, it will blossom in six weeks. If you continue to give it 18 hours at this same light intensity or somewhat higher, it will never stop blossoming. This makes it an ideal little plant to grow in the winter.

In fact, if you have a case which has a light intensity between 1200 and 1500 foot-candles, and this is not difficult for the amateur to muster, you can grow all the long-day annuals there. Some do better than others. Snapdragons were among our favorites, but the salpiglossis made the greatest hit. To our friends who were not familiar with it, they were convinced that we were growing an alpine lily.

There are other annuals that need a short day to flower well. Among them are cockscomb, cosmos, globe amaranth, salvia, and zinnia. The treatment for these is just the opposite of that which you give to long-day seedlings. If you want them to turn into bushy plants you must give them a 14-hour night.

The majority of annual and perennial seedlings are much smaller than most vegetable seedlings, so much care must be taken in transplanting them. But transplant them from the seed pot into sterilized soil just as soon as possible. Petunias and begonias, when they first show above the vermiculite, are so small they practically need to be handled with toothpicks. Use a toothpick if you must, but transplant. In spite of their tiny beginnings, most annuals grow rapidly when moved into our prepared, sterilized soil.

Annuals do better if they have a cool night with a temperature between 55 and 70 degrees Fahrenheit. The day temperature should be five to ten degrees Fahrenheit warmer.

❋ Annuals That Blossom in the Winter

Although growing annuals under lights for your summer garden is rewarding enough, growing them to blossom in your home during the winter gives you a feeling of real accomplishment. Many of the low-growing annuals can be planted in October and will be blossoming by December, and continue the winter through. Although you may enjoy many of the so-called florist plants and houseplants more, you will enjoy your favorite annuals too. Impatiens and other plants will make an outstanding and colorful display if you have a light intensity of 2000 foot-candles. Dwarf pansies, started from seed in the fall and transplanted into 4-inch pots, make interesting plants in March or April. One year we grew some particularly beautiful violas under lights.

As we have pointed out, plants are just as susceptible to temperature as to day-length. Until we realized this we were unable to grow the yellow calla lily (*Zantedeschia elliottiana*). The bulbs tended to rot and roots did not grow. Finally we gave it a 70- to 75-degree Fahrenheit night temperature and were amazed that with a 12-hour day it grew and blossomed.

We almost had to freeze the calceolaria and cineraria before they acted like florists' plants for us under lights. Once the buds had formed at a temperature below 45 degrees Fahrenheit, we put them in our long-day case and they blossomed and blossomed.

If you have a short-day case with high light intensity, the Christmas cactus is magnificent with a 10- to 12-day length. *Euphorbia fulgens*, a close sister of the poinsettia, is another delightful plant, which we grew from a cutting that we bought at Christmastime. It rooted easily under lights and blossomed several times during the year unless it was accidentally jolted by a change of temperature.

Two other southern plants, the gardenia and the bougainvillea, like a cool short-day case. Although we can't explain it, since these plants hailed from the south, the high light intensity, the short day, and the cool temperature managed to make both of these outstanding.

❀ *Perennials*

Perennials, of course, while they are seedlings, are treated exactly like annuals and vegetables. They can be grown as small plants under lights and transplanted into your flowerbed in the spring. Some will flower that season; others will not flower until the following year. On the other hand, if you have your lights in a cool place and want to use part of the space for perennials, you can start them in December or January, and oftentimes gain nearly a year. Any of the low-growing perennials can be grown in this manner.

One of our friends took slips of all the rock plants in a neighbor's garden in the summer, rooted them under lights, and grew them through the winter. In the spring she had a very fine collection of rock-garden plants, which she had grown at practically no cost: double arabis, aubrietia, pinks—a score of lovely things. When she set them out in the spring, more than half of them blossomed the first season.

Space in our lamplight greenhouse is at such a premium that we have grown only a few perennials, but their success has been outstanding. Even the lovely coral bell (*Heuchera*) blossomed, and we managed to grow delphiniums into sturdy plants without their getting so tall that we could not manage them. We have also grown some very rare aquilegia from seed.

Perhaps the best feature of growing annuals and perennials under lights is that, aside from the fact that you can have your garden filled with flowers a month earlier, you can include the best and most expensive varieties, since they are not expensive when you grow them from seed.

❀　✳　♣　❀　❀　✳　*24*

PROPAGATING

OUTDOOR PLANTS

Under artificial lights you can root cuttings from your favorite roses, dogwood, euonymus—practically any of the ornamental shrubs. We even rooted peachwood cuttings which grew into trees and bore fruit.

The consistency, constancy, and intensity of the light are the chief factors in the ease with which practically any cuttings can be rooted. It is also necessary to make a simple propagating box, and to take precautions that will prevent drying out. If attention is paid to these details success is assured.

We had always wanted to propagate our blueberries, but in spite of carefully following horticultural directions we never succeeded in rooting them. We were consoled by the fact that blueberry settings are among the most difficult to root; in fact, the taming of the wild blueberry is considered an outstanding horticultural achievement. Imagine our surprise when, after placing six hardwood cuttings of blueberries in our propagating box under artificial lights, we had three of them root in two and a half months' time! To us it was an amazing demonstration of the power of artificial light.

You can increase the number of your shrubs by means of either hardwood or softwood cuttings. A hardwood cutting is made when the leaves have fallen off, growth has stopped, and the stems have become woody. A softwood cutting is made when the stems have leaves, are green, and are in active growth. Of necessity, the amateur gardener must make his hardwood cuttings in the fall and his softwood cuttings in the summer. Hardwood cuttings root much better under artificial lights if they are made just after the leaves have fallen, in November or early December, rather than later in the year. The United States Department of Agriculture points out that "the duration of light influences the rooting of cuttings. The daylight to which the stock plant is exposed also exerts a marked effect on the ability of the cuttings to root. The woody plant *Weigela* is a good example. If grown continuously on long days, *Weigela* continues to grow and flower. Softwood cuttings can be taken anytime and these root readily under lights or in the greenhouse on the same long days. If grown on short days, less than twelve hours, the plants become quiescent and their cuttings are more difficult to root. In general too, long days provided by artificial light to extend the natural day during the rooting period cause an increase in the speed and the extent of rooting as measured by the number and length of roots produced."

🌺 *Construction of the Propagating Box*

You want to make your propagating box to fit the type of lights that will give you the greatest illumination. A good size is 13 by 41 inches with the sides 6 inches high. With such a size you can use a T-10 lamp which has an internal reflector that directs most of the light on the growth area and gives an illumination of more than 5000 foot-candles. Aside from the lights, it is simply a box; it is important, however, that the sides be about 6 inches high. Since bottom heat is the integral factor in any propagating box, you will need to buy a soil-heating cable. Dealers who sell small garden tractors usually have them, or they may be purchased from a mail-order house. These cables are available in various lengths and sizes; some are plastic-covered, others are lead-covered. Although they are more expensive, it is better to buy the lead-covered cables if you plan to use your propagating box for any length of time.

In a box the size of ours, 23 by 24 inches, a 25-foot cable fits very well. Such a cable could also be used in a box somewhat larger, or in one a little smaller. The cable is laid in spirals in the bottom of the box, with the spirals closer together near the edges, where the heat loss is highest. When you buy the soil-heating cable you will also need a special thermostat, which is sold in conjunction with it, to control the temperature of the rooting medium. These thermostats allow the current to pass through the coil when the temperature drops, and shut it off when the temperature rises.

It is also possible to regulate the temperature of the rooting medium with a variable transformer, such as children use for running their electric trains. You will not need a thermostat if such a transformer is connected to the heating coil. As the voltage is increased the temperature rises, and as the voltage is decreased the temperature drops. By placing a thermometer into the rooting medium (as deep as the base of the cuttings), you are able to adjust the system to the right temperature simply by turning the control up or down, as children do when they are running their trains fast or slowly. With this system, the coils will never need to carry more than 35 volts of electricity, whereas with the thermostat they will carry 110 to 120 volts in the circuit.

After the box is equipped with bottom heat it is filled to within about ½ inch of the top with insulating-grade vermiculite. We do not plant our cuttings directly into the rooting box but, rather, into three-quarter pots, containing about 3 inches of wet vermiculite. The pots may be of varied sizes, depending on how many cuttings you have and how tall they are. We use pots from 5 to 7 inches across. In a 5-inch pot we usually place about twenty cuttings. After the cuttings are placed in the vermiculite, the pots are sunk into the propagating box, so that their bases are practically on the soil-heating cable. Each pot is then covered with a piece of glass.

Cuttings that are to be grown under lights should be about 4 inches long. They should be taken from good stems and must have at least two leaf nodes, one that is left above the rooting medium, and one that is placed below it. (A node is a point on the stem from which a leaf springs.)

As we noted earlier, hardwood cuttings are best made right after the leaves fall in November, and should be prepared for the propagating box immediately. Rooting is encouraged by dipping the cuttings in Hormodine No. 3. Cuttings that are known to root easily need to have only the basal tip dipped, but if you have some that are difficult to root, cover about ½ inch of the lower part of the stem with the Hormodine. After being treated with Hormodine, the cutting should be placed at once in the rooting medium.

To plant the cutting, make a hole in the vermiculite with a pencil or a blunt stick. Then insert the cutting carefully so that the end does not touch the sides of the hole. This would rub off the Hormodine. After the cutting is in the hole the vermiculite is firmed around it, and glass is placed over the pot.

There are a number of advantages in this method of rooting cuttings in glass-covered pots. It is not necessary for the air surrounding the cuttings to be kept as cool as would otherwise be the case; also, the air is much more humid, an important factor in the growth of the cutting. In fact, even though the heat from the soil-heating cable, rising through the vermiculite, sometimes causes a hardwood cutting to leaf out, it does not die. Under any other circumstances, if the buds of a hardwood cutting begin to swell and unfold, its life as a cutting is over. In a glass-covered pot, even if the buds unfold, the cutting continues to grow normally and the leaves will not dry up and fall off.

The time required for a hardwood cutting to root varies. Practically every cutting we made in late November, including the blueberry, was rooted by mid-February. Some had been transplanted into soil by this time and were growing into sturdy plants.

Do not disturb the cuttings after you have planted them. It is a poor practice to lift them out to see if they have rooted. You can usually tell when the roots have formed, as the buds begin to swell and the leaves unfold and grow. At first, the effect is similar to that brought about by warm air forcing the cuttings into leaf. In that case, however, the leaves stop growing if there are no roots. With roots, the leaves continue to grow. Of course, you may have to take out an occasional cutting to examine the base, but don't make it a general practice. If the bark of a cutting turns black it is an indication that the cutting is dead.

As soon as the cuttings root, they should be transplanted into soil prepared according to the regular recipe. They continue to grow under lights until you can transplant them into a specially prepared bed out of doors in the spring. Here they will remain until they are large enough to be transplanted to their permanent locations.

❀ *Evergreen Cuttings*

Evergreen cuttings are treated exactly like other hardwood cuttings, except that it is not practical to cover them with glass; therefore they can be made considerably longer. The longer the cutting, the larger the resulting plant (a principle, however, which cannot be successfully carried too far). Broad-leafed evergreens such as the rhododendron, the azalea, the boxwood, and the euonymus, and other evergreens such as the taxus and the juniper root very quickly under lights. Evergreens should be stripped of the needles on the portion that is to be placed in the vermiculite.

Since evergreen cuttings cannot be covered with glass, it is important that they be rooted where the surrounding air is cool, preferably not over 50 to 55 degrees Fahrenheit. This keeps the buds from swelling and ensures normal rooting.

Many evergreen cuttings root in from four to six weeks. They are then planted in the regular potting soil and grown under lights until spring, when they should be set out in a plant nursery. Some will need to grow there for a year or two before they can be used as ornamental shrubs.

❀ *Softwood Cuttings*

Try to find as cool and well-ventilated a spot as possible for your lights and propagating box to root softwood cuttings in the summer. Most shrubs root more easily from softwood cuttings, although this is not a hard-and-fast rule.

You will get the best results if you keep your softwood cuttings short enough so they can be covered with a piece of glass. Plant them in exactly the same way you do the hardwood cuttings. The ends of their stems, too, should be dipped in Hormodine No. 3.

❀ *Roses*

Most of us at some time or other have tried rooting roses under an inverted jar in the garden, with very indifferent success. Perhaps that is why it is such an outstanding pleasure to root them under lights. Moreover, they not only root but grow so that you can have rosebuds in your basement nearly as easily as you can African violets.

Roses can be rooted from both hardwood and softwood cuttings, under lights, with the greatest of ease. Hardwood cuttings made in late September from healthy plants rooted in less than a month in our propagating box. They were transplanted into soil, and by the end of January were blossoming. To see the development of these 4-inch twigs that went into the propagating box pointed up the miracle of light. In May the plants were set out in the garden and blossomed during the summer.

An additional advantage of growing roses from cuttings is that a rose grown on its own roots practically never winter-kills.

Softwood cuttings taken in the summer will root in a week's time and can be set in the garden. Usually it is well to put them in a nursery bed the first year so they can be kept watered and weeded.

❀ *Fruit under Lights*

Peach Trees. Perhaps nothing illustrates more outstandingly the value of this method of rooting cuttings than the fact that we have success-fully rooted hardwood cuttings of peach trees. As far as we know, this has never been done before. These trees have always been propagated by budding on other roots. In late February we made ten 4-inch cut-tings from a Hale Haven peach. They were placed in a 7-inch pot in our propagating box, and the pot was covered with glass. By the end of a week, the bases of the cuttings had calluses, the first stage of root development in a cutting. Every one of the ten rooted within four to six weeks. These cuttings were then transplanted into our regular pot-ting soil and grew vigorously at a light intensity of about 1400 foot-candles.

Strawberries. Strawberries can be propagated and grown under

lights, which makes it possible to have some of the new and fine varieties. And of course, you can bring them in from your outdoor garden,
and enjoy them the winter through. They are particularly suited for
growing in your lamplight garden. They are low-growing plants and
hardy enough to survive the cleaning-up process necessary when you
bring any plant in from the out of doors.

In the fall, look over your everbearing strawberry plants, and select
the best-developed of the year's new runner plants for use indoors.
The spring-fruiting strawberry plants need a period of dormancy, so
they cannot be brought indoors in the fall. In January or February,
however, whenever it is possible to dig in the outdoor garden, these
early-bearing varieties may be brought indoors and grown under
lights to produce a crop of berries long before they would outside.

Strawberries are said to carry no pests. We trustingly accepted this
dictum, and did not treat with insecticides the first plants we brought
in from the garden; the spider mites came in with them. Since then we
have taken no chances. We wash the soil off the plants, examine their
roots to see that they are free from nematodes, and, while they are
bare, dip the entire strawberry plant in an Aramite solution. The plants
are then planted in sterilized soil. We put a single large plant in a
7-inch pot—or two small plants may be planted in a pot this size. In
spite of such rough treatment, our strawberry plants do not lose a leaf,
nor do they appear to be set back.

The everbearing plants usually blossom within two or three weeks
after being brought indoors and placed under lights. In order to ensure a good crop of fruit, the flowers are sprayed with Blossom-set as
soon as they have opened. Within four weeks you will have many
luscious berries.

We fertilized the plants three days after they were transplanted into
the pots, and again three days later. After that we applied fertilizer
solution once a week. The plants produced an excellent crop of berries under a 16-hour day of lamplight, and a day temperature that
averaged between 68 and 70 degrees Fahrenheit. The night temperature was about ten degrees lower.

Oranges. Orange seeds planted and grown under lights make attractive plants, but the ornamental orange, *Citrus taitentris,* is even more

attractive. It can be started easily from seeds; if you pollinate the fragrant blossoms, it will bear ornamental fruit throughout the year. It soon outgrew our greenhouse, but it continued to grow and flower under lights on the windowsill.

PROPAGATING

INDOOR PLANTS

There is nothing like a lighted niche or a new indoor greenhouse to start you on the quest for plants. Modern methods of distribution have made plants available almost everywhere. It is hard to estimate how many of these plants are sold annually, but a small plant department in a store near our home sells more than fifteen hundred plants each week at prices ranging from twenty-nine cents to four dollars and ninety-five cents.

But gardeners like to grow their own. Too, it is safer to propagate plants than it is to buy them, as it is much easier to eliminate a hidden pest from a small area than from a large one. At any rate you will want to know how it is done, for half the secret of a bushy, healthy-looking plant is youth. Most plants are lovelier at six months than are their sisters of two years, or even those of one year.

❀ *Propagating Plants from Cuttings*

Indoor plants are propagated in the same manner as outdoor ones—from seed, from rooting cuttings made from stems, from leaves, or by division.

Artificial lighting—just two fluorescent lamps or a tungsten filament bulb—will effect a complete change from your windowsill experience, where it took months before a cutting rooted. Under lights a cutting can root in a week or even in hours! We had a wandering-Jew cutting root for us in four hours, and a coleus in twenty-four, although these were exceptional.

Cuttings taken from vigorously growing plants root faster than those taken from a plant in poor condition. One cutting we made from an outdoor greenhouse—an Arthur Mallot begonia, which was growing poorly—took two months to root, and the resulting plant was anything but vigorous. On the other hand, a cutting taken from an Arthur Mallot growing vigorously under lights rooted in a week and produced a plant that sent up many side shoots. We could give you many examples, but the point is clear: don't bother to grow a cutting unless its parent plant is in good condition.

Stems that are flowering rarely make good cuttings. After they are rooted and potted they often fail to branch and instead of having an attractive bush plant, you have a rangy, straggly one.

Under artificial lights there are no seasons. A begonia roots as well in November as it does in May. It is no longer necessary to hunt up "suitable" rooting material; just turn on the faucet. You will need vermiculite only if you are growing plants from seed or rooting a leaf petiole that is very short. You will probably have some small narrow-necked vases or bottles on hand; if not you can buy 2-ounce bottles with narrow necks in a drugstore. Colored glass or opaque jars keep algae from developing, but usually under lights the cuttings root so quickly that algae don't have time to catch up with them. The neck of the container must be narrow enough to hold a short stem in water while allowing the leaves to spread out to the light in as horizontal a position as possible.

The roots of the cuttings need oxygen to develop. This was startlingly demonstrated to us by some sprays of zebrina, the red-and-silver-leafed wandering Jew, which we had placed in water in a narrow-necked blue vase 8 inches tall. After three months, only two of the eight stems in the vase had rooted, because of the lack of oxygen. We cut off the tips, placed them in 2-inch bottles, and they rooted within a week. In the shallower water, oxygen quickly reached the stems.

As water is absorbed by the plants, and also evaporates, it is necessary to keep an eye on these small containers, for the water must be replenished frequently. If the water dries up, the cutting will have a serious setback and may die.

For generations, cuttings have been the "friendship chain." If, while visiting a friend, you express admiration for the vigor and growth of his plants and he graciously replies, "I'll give you a slip," the best response is to whip out a razor blade. Make a clean cut of a branch of the plant, one with four leaf nodes, if possible. If you are not foresighted enough to have a razor blade, a clean knife will do; or, lacking that, the branch can be broken off and pruned later. The cut is made crosswise across the stem, just below a leaf node.

On the windowsill the tip of the stem grows much better than any other portion of the plant, but under the lights it doesn't seem to matter what part of the stem you use, providing it is correctly prepared. Long stems are not good. One that is 4 or 5 inches long is the best; however, we have rooted short 2-inch cuttings under lights with no difficulty.

Some horticulturists give a general rule: leave as many leaves on a cutting as will not wilt. But the rule is hard for the amateur to interpret. Where is the dividing line between wilting and nonwilting leaves? A more workable rule is to make your cuttings so that each one has four leaves attached to a clean-cut stem. Remove the two bottom leaves and place the stem in water so that two leaf nodes are covered. Let the two upper leaves stretch out to the light.

Many kinds of plants can be propagated from stem cuttings with the aid of artificial lights. Stem cuttings from petunias, asters, chrysanthemums, geraniums, and coleus, as well as a score of other garden favorites, may be made in the fall and rooted under lights. They will grow into beautiful plants under 500 foot-candles of light, and they will blossom under 1000 to 1500 foot-candles.

However, you do not need that high a light intensity to root stem cuttings. Many plants can be propagated from stem cuttings, under a 20-watt fluorescent tube, 4 or 5 inches above the propagating bottle, or under a 60-watt incandescent bulb in a reflector 18 inches above the plants. Those were the lights we used in the experiment, almost at the beginning of our work with growing plants under lights. We used a list of plants given in a Cornell University pamphlet, *Plants and Flowers in the Home*, by Kenneth Post. We located cuttings from practically all the plants mentioned, and every single one grew. You can grow them, too, under whatever light you have at hand:

Agave	Crown-of-Thorns	Lantana
Ageratum	Cuphea	Nephthytis
Aglaonema	Dieffenbachia	Pandanus
Aloe	Dracaena	Peperomia
Anthurium	Erica	Petunia
Azalea	Gardenia	Pilea
Begonia	Genista	Poinsettia
Beloperone	Geranium	Rhoco
Cactus	German Ivy	Solanum
Calceolaria	Gynura	Stephanotis
Chrysanthemum	Hedera	Tolmiea
Cissus	Hydrangea	Tradescantia
Citrus	Impatiens	Vinca
Coleus	Iresine	Zebrina
Crassula	Kalanchoe	Zygocactus

But though these cuttings can be started under these lights, they need much more light intensity to grow. Actually their light requirements vary greatly. If your indoor greenhouse has a light intensity between 1000 and 1500 foot-candles, most of these plants not only will grow but will need to be pinched back. Pinching, as any gardener can tell you, consists of removing the tip of a plant, as soon as it has four to six leaves, by snipping it off with your thumbnail (though, of course, a knife may be used instead). Side shoots can be pinched off and encouraged to branch more fully as soon as four or five leaf nodes have developed.

Lopping off these leaves is the only way you are going to get an attractive plant. You need to cut or pinch off both the side branches and the basal branches, and you may have to do it again and again. This pinching makes the difference between having a round, compact plant, and having a gangling one that shoots up and touches the lights.

Begonias, calceolarias, fuchsias, and poinsettias must be pinched from the very beginning.

❈ Propagating Plants by Division

Dividing plants to increase the population of a perennial border is a familiar practice to most gardeners. The same method may be used to increase the number of plants in your indoor garden. The procedure is identical. Only plants which send up shoots from the roots can be divided, such as ferns and the semperflorens begonia. Shake off some of the dirt, and break or cut the plant apart with a dull knife between the sections where stems have come up through the soil. Make sure that roots are attached to each one of the stems, and try to divide the plant as evenly as possible. If you wind up with a small root section and a large quantity of leaves, trim off some of the leaves to balance the roots. Sometimes there will be so few roots that you will be able to save only a few leaves. But this need not discourage you. Under artificial lights very small sections grow quickly into large-sized plants.

Rhizomatous begonias and the ferns that have rhizomes are the easiest of all plants to divide because just a short section of the rhizome and a few leaves will form a plant. If the rhizome has no roots, it will quickly develop some if placed in water. Leave part of the rhizome out of the water, for if it is entirely submerged it will not root.

The Boston fern can be divided by simply cutting the single plant apart and putting each section in a separate pot. A large plant will give you four or five smaller ones. Ferns also send up tiny new shoots, usually at the edges of their pots. These shoots may be removed and planted in small pots. Soon they will unfurl husky new fronds. This is the common method of reproducing the Boston fern and its many relatives.

The strawberry geranium (*Saxifraga*) and the spider lily (*Chlorophytum*) also send out shoots on which small plants develop. Unlike the Boston fern, they reproduce plants in air. It is not necessary for any of their tips to touch the moist earth before they can reproduce new plantlets. These shoots with the tiny plants attached are known as runners. They do not develop roots, however, unless they can anchor themselves to the soil; but if they are removed from the mother plant and placed in water, within a few days roots will develop. They are then ready to be potted in soil.

Reproduction by plant division occurs in another form when bulbous plants naturally form small bulblets, which can be removed and planted. The spring-flowering bulbs—tulips, hyacinths, and narcissus—are in this class, as are the clivia freesia, amaryllis, oxalis, the achimenes, and many others.

❀ *Plants from Offshoots*

Small plants that develop at the base of a larger one are called offshoots. Some begonias, African violets, dracaenas, the screw pine, and numerous other plants produce offshoots. Most of these can be rooted in water, just as stem cuttings are rooted. However, when the stem is too short to stay in water, it may be necessary to resort to vermiculite as a rooting medium. All that is necessary is to keep the offshoot moist while the roots are developing.

The only disappointment we ever had in our rooting experiments under artificial lights was when we tried to propagate the offshoots of the dracaena and the screw pine in this manner. Instead of rooting, they died. Now, when an offshoot appears on either of these plants, we pack a little dirt around the small plant where it joins the main stem. In this extra earth the offshoot will develop roots of its own, and in a short time you can remove it without fear of damaging it. Since both of these plants are much more attractive when they are young than when they are older, it is wise to propagate the young plants as soon as they appear.

These plants can also be encouraged to form by air-layering. This means that a slit is made at about a 45-degree angle in the side of the stem, 6 inches from the tip, and quite deep, almost three-quarters through the stem. The cut is held open with a toothpick, and sphagnum moss is wrapped around the wound you have made. The sphagnum moss must be kept moist—difficult to remember, but absolutely essential. A piece of polyethylene plastic (like the plastic vegetable bags), wrapped around the moss and secured with string, will help to retain the moisture. Quite soon roots will start to grow where the stem has been cut. The stem is then cut off below the moss, and the new plant started in soil. Not only dracaenas can be reproduced in this manner; rubber plants, dieffenbachias, and the dracaena palm propagate well from air-layering.

❀ Plants from Leaves

The list of plants which can be propagated from leaves is not long. The most familiar is the African violet, but there are others, especially among the begonias. The rex, the star, and the Christmas begonia can invariably be grown by this means, although it is easier for the amateur to root the last from a stem cutting. The procedure is the same one used in propagating African violets, except that, with the larger leaves, you need a longer stem. The jade plant, the peperomia, the gloxinia, and the piggy-back plant can also be rooted from leaves, although here, too, you may prefer to propagate them by means of a stem cutting.

The piggy-back plant is difficult to root in water, since it must touch the surface of the water at the exact point where the little plant is growing on the larger leaf; it is best rooted in vermiculite. The petiole should be about 1½ inches long. This is pushed into the vermiculite until the leaf touches the surface. If the vermiculite is kept properly moistened, the leaf will root in a short time. As soon as it does, it can be potted in soil. The rooting of leaves from the African violet is discussed in Chapter 28.

GROWING YOUR
SALAD GREENS

In the fall and winter you may prefer to use your greenhouse lights for growing a continuous succession of vegetables for your salad bowl, rather than to use them for producing beautiful, flowering houseplants. It is not difficult or costly to achieve the needed light intensity, for in growing these vegetables you are seeking foliage—not flowers—so fluorescent tubes may be hung close above the tops of the plants; if necessary, they can be as close as 4 or 6 inches.

For the homemaker, such an arrangement is an excellent auxiliary to the freezer. And once you have proudly picked a basement-grown head of Boston lettuce or reveled in the tangy taste of freshly cut Bibb, you will talk in superlatives. Perhaps because of their rarity, as we eat the leaves of lettuce we have grown under fluorescent tubes—Boston, white cos, Bibb, and New York State iceberg—we insist that they taste much better when picked in December than they do when picked in June.

In these days of gourmet cooking, you'll be surprised what fresh vegetables grown under lights can do for your table. They really take less time than making stock from ham bones and turkey stripped down, and are considerably more original. These little bits of flavor, if you combine them carefully, add up to a magnificent whole.

Just try washing a pot of baby carrots so they are gleaming gold, add a few chopped radishes (about a quarter of a pot, let the others grow till next time) into a tossed salad of fresh-grown lettuce, a few leaves of endive, chopped celery leaves, and basil. It tastes so good your guests will all want to grow their salads under lights. Even if they never get to do it, they will tell everyone how *you* do.

It's the same way with the vegetable seedlings that you grow for your garden out of doors. They are so much bushier, healthier, and larger than most seedlings that one can buy that everyone talks of growing theirs under lights.

Vegetables, whether ready for the garden or only a day or two old, are as individual in their preferences and habits as any flower. Some like warm surroundings, and some become spindly almost overnight in a temperature of over 70 degrees Fahrenheit. Eggplant, squash, melons, peppers, cucumbers, and tomatoes prefer a warmer temperature than that wanted by other vegetable seedlings. However, in a day temperature of 60 to 70 degrees Fahrenheit, and a somewhat lower night temperature, both cool-loving and warm-loving vegetables grow well for us in a light intensity of 1000 foot-candles.

If you have grown vegetables in the house all winter, you will easily be able to tell how far ahead the different ones should be planted to be ready to go in the garden when danger of frost is past. If you have never seen how fast they grow, you may be tempted to plant them too early. In the average amateur indoor greenhouse, five weeks ahead of time is usually a safe figure.

Since seedlings need a large amount of light, give them an 18-hour day if you have a timer. They will also grow well with just 16 hours of light. This makes it possible to operate the cases manually if necessary.

The growing of many vegetables has already been mentioned in speaking of vegetables for your winter use, but the notes in this chapter on growing a number of vegetable seedlings should prove helpful.

Asparagus. If you are interested in a good asparagus bed, you can start one with little trouble under artificial lights. Seeds will germinate in 13 to 14 days, and they immediately grow strong radicles. Asparagus is noted for its roots, as anyone who has tried to uproot a well-established plant will testify. Give the day-old seedling plenty of

You can have flowers in your window garden even when there is not too much winter sunshine if you conceal two Power-Groove coolwhite tubes behind the valance.

African violets show the effect of different daily rations in hours of exposure to artificial lights and light intensities. (*Photos courtesy General Electric*)

100 Fc   300 Fc   600 Fc

Orchid Wonder
6 hours

27292

100 Fc   300 Fc   600 Fc

Orchid Wonder
12 hours

27292-A

100 Fc   300 Fc   600 Fc

Orchid Wonder
18 hours

27292-B

(Photos courtesy U.S. Department of Agriculture)

Seeds of bromeliads. *Left:* Seeds kept without light. *Right:* Seeds which have received eight hours of light per day for several days.

Poinsettia plants which have received (left to right) eight, nine, eleven, and twelve hours of light a day.

Student working in the North Carolina State University phytotron. Specular aluminum-lined controlled environment rooms supply plants with about 260 watts of fluorescent and incandescent light per square foot. (*Photo courtesy Dr. R. J. Downs*)

The effect of carbon dioxide on the growth of plants is dramatically demonstrated in this photograph. Both petunia seedlings are six weeks old. The one on the left was grown in a greenhouse under ordinary conditions. The one on the right was treated with carbon dioxide in the atmosphere during the day. (*Photo courtesy U. S. Department of Agriculture*)

Two types of growing lamps which may be used on any table or shelf. (*Top photo courtesy of Craft House, Wilson, N.Y.; bottom photo courtesy of Floralite Company*)

Top: A Floraliter lighted tray is a handsome addition to any room. *Bottom:* Lights over a simple bench will grow flowers in any part of the house. (*Photos courtesy House Plant Corner, Oxford, Md.*)

Orchids and African violets grow well together in a light intensity of 1000 foot-candles. The lady's slipper at the right is *Cypripedium* variety Jacqueline Kranz. (*Photo by Frederick H. Kranz*)

A four-inch cutting of the floribunda rose, Chatter, taken in October, was transformed into a bush with ten full-blown roses by late March. (*Photo by Frederick H. Kranz*)

Vegetables flourish with automatic watering, supplied through the pipe in the foreground. Pots rest on pans filled with vermiculite. (*Photo by Frederick H. Kranz*)

room for root development by transplanting to a 3-inch pot. When we planted asparagus seed in early January under a light intensity of 1000 foot-candles, it produced strong feathery stems, 8 inches tall, by March. These seedlings can be set out of doors as soon as you have a place prepared for them. You will find that, at the end of a year, you have a finer asparagus bed than if you had purchased two-year-old plants.

Basil, sweet. Although the clovelike taste of basil leaves is an interesting addition to a winter salad, the plant grows slowly and is quite spindly, even under a light intensity of 1400 foot-candles. It almost seems more worthwhile to use the space for more vigorous, if less pungent, herbs.

Beets, see *Carrots.*

Broccoli. Broccoli can cause you trouble under lights because it grows so rapidly. In eight weeks you will have a well-leafed plant a foot tall. It would keep right on growing if you could give it headspace. It will withstand quite cool weather, so you can transplant it to the outdoor garden between April 25 and May 15 (depending on when springlike weather arrives in your area).

Brussels sprouts. Brussels sprouts, like all members of the cabbage family, are easily grown under lights. Even under a two-tubed fluorescent lamp, you can produce excellent plants for your outdoor garden.

Cabbage. Cabbage grows with the same ease and vigor under lights as does lettuce, as long as you keep the temperature between 60 and 65 degrees Fahrenheit (though it can be lower); cabbage will grow well even under a low light intensity. The seeds should be planted seven to nine weeks before the plants are to be set out in the garden.

Cabbage plants are very hardy, so they are among the vegetables you can transplant early. As soon as they are adjusted, light frosts will not injure them.

See also *Chinese cabbage.*

Carrots and Beets. It is fun to grow a few carrots indoors in winter, but it's not practical to start them for the outdoor garden. The same is true of beets. Both vegetables can be planted outdoors as soon as the ground can be worked, and, though they germinate slowly, once started, they grow rapidly. Neither can be transplanted successfully without the greatest care, for if the long, tender taproots are broken, you get small and malformed produce. But when the snow is flying, the garden-freshness of tender carrots and round young beets that you have grown yourself under lights is another matter.

In a 5-inch pot you can plant the equivalent of a "bunch," and in two to two and a half months you will be able to "dig" them. Carrots grow rapidly, so if you have a variety that is long and slender you will need a 7-inch pot. If the tip of the carrot touches the bottom of the pot, it curls and fails to develop normally.

Cauliflower. You can count on having good cauliflower plants if you start them under lights. Within eight to ten weeks after the seeds germinate, you will have sturdy, broad-leafed plants that will give you excellent early heads. Cabbage (see above) and cauliflower seeds may be planted at the same time, but keep the cauliflower seedlings under the lights about two weeks longer. This gives you plants that are somewhat larger. Cauliflower is not quite as hardy as cabbage, so transplanting it to the outdoor garden ten days to two weeks later is a wise precaution.

Celery. With celery it is especially important to have good seed, not only to produce a quality crop, but to ensure good germination. Celery seeds should be sown about the last week in February in the northern states. We transplant the seedlings into 2½-inch pots, where they grow with vigor. Celery requires as much coddling in cold weather as do tomatoes. Because it is so sensitive to cold, try to adjust the plants to the out of doors gradually, bringing them back indoors at night for nearly a week, and be careful to keep them well watered.

Under lights celery grows so normally that you can raise it during the winter. The Early Pascal is vigorous and makes a good leafy plant.

Chinese cabbage. This is one of the hardiest of salad plants. You can head it under a light intensity of 1000 to 1500 foot-candles, but you can also grow it in your living room and have good-sized tangy leaves to give real zest to your winter salads. We decided that it made a much prettier houseplant than the aspidistra and the dracaena, so we prepared a pot with a wick and placed it, with Chinese cabbage growing in it, under our living-room lights. When it reached the proper size, it was cut up for salad and a new one took its place. The only disadvantage in such a system is that you have a certain uncomfortable feeling, chopping it so ruthlessly. In the living room, it comes into the family circle.

Curly endive, see *Endive*.

Cucumbers. Cucumbers grow well under lights, provided you give them a warm enough temperature. A single plant that we grew in our living room under a two-tubed fluorescent arrangement grew a series of tiny pickling-sized fruit in each leaf axil at the end of five weeks from the date of germination. In our cool bedroom, where the temperature was between 55 and 60 degrees Fahrenheit, the leaves yellowed and the plant grew poorly in spite of a somewhat better light intensity. Like so many of the vine vegetables, cucumbers grown under lights like a temperature of at least 75 degrees.

Cucumbers grow so rapidly that, in growing them for the garden, it is better not to plant the seeds until four weeks before you expect to set the seedlings out of doors.

It is possible to grow cucumbers for the table under your lights in the winter, if you care to take the trouble. The vine of a single plant may be trained on a string which is run close to the lights, thus giving the plant the light and heat it likes. You will have to pollinate the blossoms and it is most important to give the plants plenty of fertilizer and water. If you fail to get delicious, crisp cucumbers, it will be because you have been lax in pollinating or watering. While fruiting, cucumber plants require an enormous amount of water.

The easiest way to pollinate the flowers is to buy a specially prepared hormone which causes fruit to set. It is sold under the name of Blossom-set, and can be obtained from practically all garden-supply houses. It should be diluted and used according to directions given on the bottle. You apply it as a spray, using a perfume atomizer, on the freshly opened pistillate flowers (which produce the cucumbers). You can recognize these, as each is attached to a miniature cucumber. Blossom-set can also be purchased packaged in aerosol bombs, and used without further preparation.

Eggplants. Eggplants grow exceptionally well under lights in a temperature of 60 to 70 degrees Fahrenheit, and are ready for the garden in early June if they have been planted under lights in mid-February. The seedlings can be placed in 2-inch bands or 2½-inch pots, and a little later can be transferred to 4-inch pots. Even if the fruit has started to set under lights, it continues to grow in the garden. It is most important, however, not to let the plants become potbound or dried out. This stunts their growth so that they never make good garden plants. When the weather becomes warm, adjust the plants to the out of doors gradually, so they will not be hardened or set back.

Endive, curly. Also known as chicory, this plant grows somewhat more slowly than lettuce, but if you are fond of its bitter-sweetness you will feel it is worth giving up space to under the lights for eight to ten weeks while it forms a large, loose-leafed head. And, of course, you can begin by eating the outer leaves, letting the main plant continue to produce for a month or more.

Lettuce. Lettuce will grow as leaf lettuce if several plants are placed in one pot, or planted close together in a flat. However, you can get a good head in from six to nine weeks if you transplant directly from the seed pan to a 4-inch pot. Frequent transplanting sets lettuce back. It also needs lots and lots of water. If the soil becomes the least bit dry, the outer leaves dry up and turn brown, and you'll want to be able to eat every single leaf. In addition to using automatic watering, you may need to give your lettuce extra water with your watering can once or twice a week. At any rate, keep your eye on the soil. Too, like any other rapid-growing plant, lettuce must be regularly fertilized (twice a week or more) or the leaves will turn yellow. We analyzed the soil for nitrogen in some of the pots of lettuce we had been fertilizing just once a week. The plants were growing so fast that practically no nitrogen was left; it was down to the low count of 5 parts per 1,000,000. We also found that, under lights, lettuce grows better if the pots are crowded close together. It seems to help prevent the soil from drying out.

Boston lettuce grows faster than any of the other varieties we grew including New York State iceberg, Bibb, and cos. It heads faster, too, an important factor when you are eating a pot of it each day.

Lettuce comes quickly to edible maturity under a light intensity of 1000 foot-candles or more. With a lesser light intensity the plants and leaves will be small and will fail to head. Its one added requirement is constant and sufficient moisture. With good light and proper moisture you can grow excellent heads of lettuce throughout the winter. Boston is the most satisfactory, since it grows easily and forms a head faster than the other varieties. For a continuous supply, sow new seeds about every two to four weeks.

New York State iceberg is our second choice; it quickly grows large-sized leaves, but is difficult to keep moist enough indoors. The outer leaves will dry out, too, if the humidity in your indoor greenhouse drops too much. Bibb and white cos likewise grow well under lights, but are slower than the first two.

In growing lettuce for the garden, set the plants out of doors when the leaves are about 2½ inches long, and be sure to keep them well watered.

Muskmelons. To make certain of a good crop of muskmelons, the seeds must be started indoors not later than the end of March. The seeds come up quickly, and you will have to keep a close watch on them so the plants won't overrun your indoor greenhouse. As soon as all danger of frost is past, set them in a well-prepared hill. The greatest hazard in growing melons is root injury. You can avoid it by transplanting the seedlings into 4-inch pots at the first transplanting from the seed pan. Before filling the pot with soil, place a large fragment of broken pot over the drainhole, so the ball of earth can be pushed out of the pot easily when you are ready to place the muskmelon plant in the outdoor garden. If the roots are injured, the plant usually dies.

Onions. Onions must be started in January or February to produce good, mature plants to set out in the garden in May. Onions are among the vegetables that especially like growing under the lights. Five or six can be grown in a 5-inch pot. Under a light intensity of 1000 foot-candles (or slightly more), onions will grow as though they were in an outdoor garden in midsummer. However, they can do with less light; we grew some under the fluorescent lamp in our living room, with a light intensity of only 650 foot-candles. At the end of five weeks, however, they should have been transplanted to the garden, for they were not as vigorous as their relatives that were being grown under a greater light intensity; they flopped over with little provocation. Sweet Spanish onions, the White Globe, and leeks were grown under our lights with uniform success. By starting the sweet Spanish onion from seed in January, you will have bulbs so large that, when they are gathered in the fall, they will not fit into a 2-quart saucepan without being quartered. Spanish onions can be planted in the garden as soon as the weather permits you to prepare a place for them.

Long hours of lamplight encourage onion seedlings to grow as "spring onions." Under a light cycle of 10 to 12 hours, the bulbs will enlarge.

Parsley. Many gardeners have lifted parsley from the outdoor garden and had it continue to grow somewhat weakly on the windowsill. Parsley grown from seed under lights acts quite differently, and is an interesting addition to your winter garden. We transplant the seedlings to a 3-inch pot, and from only a few plants have garnish throughout the winter. Parsley seems a little weak when first transplanted, but within a month will be growing vigorously under the lights.

If you are growing it for the garden, sow the seeds during the first week of March, and the seedlings will be ready for outdoor planting when the weather permits.

Peppers. Pepper seeds are said to keep their fertility for four years —and longer if they are kept in the pods—but one year we had difficulty in securing good seeds. They should be sown in late February. It takes from 10 to 20 days for the seeds to germinate; they are then transplanted into 3-inch pots.

Pepper plants are delicate, and must be carefully adjusted to the out of doors before being planted in the garden. Drying out stunts their growth badly.

Radishes. Radishes can be grown as quickly and easily under 1000 foot-candles of light as they can out of doors. We transplant about five seedlings into a 4-inch pot; within six weeks they are 1 inch in diameter.

Squash. Squash grows so fast under artificial lights that it wears out its welcome in most indoor greenhouses. For both its sake and yours, do not start it too early. If the plants become stunted for any reason, they are useless. They must not become potbound, and if they develop a large number of blossoms they are usually poor plants for the garden. They grow best in a warm temperature—between 65 and 75 degrees Fahrenheit—and even at this high temperature they can survive on very little light (650 foot-candles). Like melons and eggplants, they will continue to grow rampantly if you succeed in transplanting them without injuring their roots. Squash seedlings should be transplanted into 4-inch pots.

Sweet basil, see *Basil*.

Tomatoes. Tomatoes are the plants most people really want to grow under artificial lights and, fortunately, this plant is eminently suited for growing in this manner. Although you can start the plants with a light intensity of 1000 to 1400 foot-candles, they do best with more, as much as 2500 foot-candles in order to fruit abundantly. They must also be staked and grown in a very large pot with automatic watering so that the soil is always moist. Like cucumbers, they must be fertilized twice a week, and grown in a temperature of at least 70 or 75 degrees Fahrenheit. If you give four plants this kind of care, you can have your own home-grown tomatoes all winter long.

You can start tomato plants for your garden under a two-tubed fluorescent lamp, but you will get spindly plants if you grow them there for longer than two or three weeks. If you plan to set out the plants by the last week in May, they should be transplanted from the seed pan into 3-inch pots by the tenth of April. If they are fertilized regularly, kept constantly moist, and carefully prevented from being potbound, tomato plants can be grown under lights until they blossom. If these are adapted to the garden carefully and gradually, they will produce early tomatoes. Continue to water them until they become acclimated to the out of doors.

Watercress. Watercress, too, grows rapidly under lights, provided you give it enough water. In an effort to keep one of our plants from drying out, we finally set it in a bowl of water for half an hour a day. This single plant soaked up a cup of water a day and flourished.

You will greatly speed the time needed for your vegetables if you treat them often to carbon dioxide. A cucumber, for example, was edible six weeks after it germinated when carbon dioxide was introduced into the case every day.

PART IV

Now You Can Grow . . .

27

ORCHIDS

Orchids are exotic and expensive, beautiful and fleeting, and grow under lights in a tantalizing, successful, frustrating way. It sometimes seems their behavior is most unscientific in what appears to be carefully controlled conditions. Perhaps what really makes an orchid fancier is the fact that it is so hard to master the orchid's beguiling ways. In fact, orchids so captivate the people who grow them that orchid growers are rarely interested in growing anything else.

The first hurdle is finding a plant. Florists look at you incredulously when you say that you would like to buy an orchid, and then you shake your head when they bring out a beautiful purple spray of vandas or a single white cattleya. You often prove to be the first customer they have met who wanted an orchid *plant*. Flowers come by air to northern cities, but not plants. In all probability you'll have to order by mail.

It is probably because orchids are expensive and different that their owners refer to them as "orchid collections." Indeed, some collections have been sold for as much as twenty-five thousand dollars. This fact makes growing orchids sound almost like an investment. It is, but it's not a monetary one. Orchids that have been given a First Class Certificate or an Award of Merit by the American or British orchid societies often command high prices, but you can buy an orchid plant of certain species for five dollars or less, and if your zeal is great, you may also grow orchid seedlings. In the process you have all the fun of growing very challenging flowers successfully. That is the dividend of growing them under lights.

Although orchids are sometimes difficult to flower, they have what might be considered an iron constitution. When plant explorers discovered orchids in the late 1700s in Central and South America, the plants were shot down from trees, carried from the jungles by slow means of transportation, shipped on sailing vessels to England—yet they still managed to survive. Orchid fanciers have been growing them ever since. It is estimated there are some twenty thousand species, plus innumerable hybrids.

Enthusiastic orchid growers tend to divide orchids into two classes, the florist's orchids and the species orchids. Most growers start with those that florists sell. The most familiar are those of the *Cattleya* genus, the beautiful purple or white orchids that bespeak special occasions. Growers try to help you with the strange nomenclature by calling cattleyas "catts," cypripediums "lady's slippers," and miltonias "pansy orchids"; yet it isn't long before you prefer to use the scientific names.

Although you may begin with the growing of the so-called florists' orchids, you will gradually become interested in the species orchids, which can be equally beautiful and are imported from all parts of the earth. You can even become an importer yourself by writing to the United States Department of Agriculture, Bureau of Entomology and Plant Quarantine, Hoboken, New Jersey. They will give you a number, tags, and directions, which you must have in order to import plants. It's very simple, and exciting as well, to get orchids from dealers in India, in South America, in England.

You will find the names of dealers, and, what is equally important, stories of various individuals' experiences in growing orchids in the bulletins of the two orchid societies.* There, too, are published pic-

* The American Orchid Society's *Bulletin* comes with membership in the society. The address is Botanical Museum of Harvard University, Cambridge, Mass. The English publication is *The Orchid Review*, Buxted Park Gardens, North Uckfield, Sussex, England.

tures of orchids that have won awards, as well as articles on developments in the orchid field.

It is practically impossible to tell you what orchids to grow. In a sense you grow what orchids you can get.

One time when we had seen photographs of a dozen or more orchids that had won a Certificate of Cultural Merit from the American Orchid Society, we carefully copied their names. They were so beautiful that we decided those were the orchids we would grow. We found only one, *Dendrobium anosmum*. The specimen plant was unbelievably lovely, but the seedling we finally rounded up, in spite of our loving care, simply died. Strangely enough, we have never been very successful with the dendrobiums.

We tended to shy away from the tall orchids. We never did succeed in blossoming a cymbidium under lights. Our daughter was more successful, growing the plants we gave her on the windowsill during the winter and out of doors all summer and far into the fall. It meant carrying them indoors and out during October and part of November, and there were always disasters. The temperature would drop to 28 degrees Fahrenheit some nights—and the cymbidiums had not been brought in! There was that never-forgotten first cymbidium to flower from a seedling that was in full bud out of doors for a day, when one of the children's horses gobbled it up. They had tethered him too close to our prize.

Our favorite orchids are the cypripediums, the lady's-slipper orchids. They do not require as high a light intensity as many. They blossom for us in a case with African violets and begonias.

We like *Epidendrum cochleatum*, too. It is not as showy as many, but it pleases us to grow the first orchid ever imported into Europe. Further, it has proved to be almost ever-flowering, at as low a light intensity as 750 foot-candles.

Of course, you will have your favorites too. Orchids have something of both fairy and goblin in their makeup. Some orchids that others found hard to grow proved easy for us, while some of the "easy orchids" just never flowered at all. Always there were the rewards of the unexpected; a new lead (or growth) on a bulb that hardly looked as though it would grow; a letter from a friend we had

never met attached to a carefully wrapped package with some mil-
tonia seedlings that he had grown from seed; or a blossom suddenly
appearing on a species plant that takes you on mental wings to the
Andes, to Mexico, to the monsoon sweeps of Asia.

You will need to use a special mixture because orchids do not like
soil. There are probably more recipes for mixtures in which to grow
orchids than there are for African violets. In different orchid publications you can read absolutely contrary statements as to the best way
to grow an orchid. The question really is not what they will grow in,
since orchids seem to grow in anything after a fashion. The real test is
how well they grow and how soon they will flower.

We have grown some species orchids in peat moss, carefully sifted
so that mostly fibers are left and combined with charcoal in the ratio
of 2 parts peat moss to 1 part charcoal. We prepare the charcoal by
sifting it on a wire screen, 6 wires to the inch. Then on a screen with 2
wires to the inch, and again on the 6-to-the-inch screen. With all this
sifting there is not so much left for the orchids.

Actually there are better mediums in which to grow orchids. We
were quite successful in growing some odontoglossum seedlings in this
mixture as a base with 1 cup each of vermiculite and coarse perlite,
and 1 teaspoonful of whiting added. In fact, in spite of the rigors of an
air journey at an early age, *Odontoglossum cruentum x Odontoglossum tordonia* flowered in two years from the time we received it, a
seedling just out of a flask, in this mixture.

The time-honored substance for growing orchids is osmunda or
osmundine—the roots of the osmunda fern—which is sold in bales. It is
in short supply in this country, but it can be imported from Japan and
Italy, and you may be able to find a dealer who sells it. Tree-fern, tan-
bark, and sphagnum moss are also favored by dealers, used either
alone or in combination with other substances.

Most osmunda contains a considerable quantity of fine dust from
decayed leaves and other materials. It comes in such a mat of inte-
grated roots that it is often difficult to pull apart. It is important to
have the fibers clean so that the other materials will not clog the drainage process in the pot. We first cut the osmunda into 6- or 8-inch
squares and work with them until the dirt is eliminated. We use tin-
snips in the beginning. Then we cut the fibers into 4- to 6-inch

lengths, using a paper-cutter. If the pieces are still dirty, they are placed on window screen and shaken until the dirt falls through. We store the osmunda in these 4- to 6-inch lengths, but actually when we use them in potting an orchid, we cut them with the paper-cutter into 2-inch and 1-inch lengths, which are kept separate and used with different species. The roots of cattleyas tend to go right through the medium so the entire pot is filled with branching roots. That is why it is necessary to leave the osmunda fibers longer in potting cattleyas and not pack them too tightly. However with cypripediums the fibers should be 1 inch in length. If you have not grown these orchids, and have not carefully studied the root-growth habits, you might well question the importance of different lengths of osmunda fiber. We found it made a great difference in the way the plants grew.

Potting an orchid properly is an art you must master. Drainage is all-important. It will help you if your orchids rest on a wire screen so the water will drain through rapidly. This hinges on proper potting. You begin by dealing with the drainage in the bottom of the pot. We have found that if you use broken pieces of pots with a section of the rim still attached, you can quite easily make a tentlike arrangement of these pieces over the hole in the bottom. Slope them toward the bottom but close enough together so stones can't come in between them, and protect them with two more pieces like a tent-fly. Over these you put ½ inch of round stones (the colored stones for an aquarium work very well).

After this ground work has been done, you turn to the orchid you are planning to pot. If there are any old, dead brown roots, cut them away. Some orchids have brown roots naturally, but most orchid roots are whitish; just be sure the roots you are cutting off are dead. Roots on cattleyas frequently die, and if they are not removed they clog the drainage.

In picking the pot size for your orchid, be sure that the roots will fit in it easily and don't need to be twisted around the pot. Before you put the plant in the pot, pack the osmunda and charcoal between the roots of the plant while you hold it upside down. Your aim is to work to develop short, small roots, as these hold more water.

Then you put the plant with its stuffed roots into the pot. Holding it in position, you add a layer of chopped osmunda alternating with the charcoal. The charcoal should be in small pieces and sifted on a screen so the dirt is completely removed. You end with the charcoal on top. By this method of potting orchids, we found the soil tended to stay neutral. We tested fifteen plants potted in this manner after they had been growing for six months, and all but one tested neutral. The one was pH 6.4.

You can test your potting ability and the soil you have by slowly pouring water into the pot. If the water runs right through, you have a soil that orchids can live with very pleasantly.

Perhaps the most important skill is that of watering the plants properly. If watering is an art with most plants, with orchids it is even more: an art, a science, and something of an emotional experience. When you water an orchid everything must be wetted. The compost needs to dry out before it is watered again. We found it necessary to water our orchids every twenty-four hours, even though the relative humidity in the case was 60 per cent.

The theory is that the drying out of the compost brings in fresh air; the plant roots consume something from the air and grow.

If you train your fingers, you can learn to test the medium to see if it is thoroughly dry or not by touching it. This may not sound difficult, but there's a difference between slightly wet, dry, and thoroughly dry, and the optimum is the last-named. But you want to avoid "bone dry." Another way to test for dryness is to examine the color of the osmunda fiber. The dryer the fiber the lighter it is.

Although the general practice in starting a collection of orchids is to buy mature plants, they invariably arrive with bare roots. We usually plunge them into a pail of water for twenty-four hours before planting them. Orchids freeze easily, so avoid ordering plants at any time when it is cold or there is danger of a frost. You may decide, instead, to grow your own plants from seed.

It takes scientific skill to germinate orchid seeds successfully. For a long time their germination was a botanical mystery. Occasionally a grower would be successful when he planted seed in the ground under a growing plant. A symbiotic fungus present there would encourage germination. But orchid seedlings were not easy to grow until scientists learned how they could be grown on agar in a sterilized flask.

But even under the best of circumstances there are difficulties. It is easier to buy seedlings just out of a flask, or even in a flask, from recognized dealers.

Artificial lights make the growing of these seedlings an almost certain success. The seedlings that you buy from a flask are usually between a half an inch and an inch in height. We put our seedlings into sterilized growing mixtures, chopped osmunda fiber and specially sifted peat moss and charcoal. The pot is covered with glass and put close to the lights in a temperature of 78 degrees Fahrenheit at night, 10 degrees higher during the day. We have never lost a seedling and the speed with which they develop into sizable plants is amazing. If you water them with almost hot water, they seem to grow better than with lukewarm. Caring for them as you would a baby ensures good plants.

You will be surprised to notice that there is a great difference in the vigor of growth of seedlings from the same flask. After about three months, we transplant the seedlings from the community pot, as it is called, into 4-inch pots, with six seedlings in each. You will note that the vigorous growers usually continue to hold their own. You will want nonetheless to grow all the seedlings until they flower since seedlings from the same flask can differ greatly. Some will be much lovelier than others, and one of the slow growers may prove to be a prize-winner.

Our most exciting flowering of an orchid seedling was a cypripedium, which we bought from Peter Black, one of the great orchid growers in England. It usually takes seven years to flower a cypripedium, but this flowered for us in less than half the time. It was the first cypripedium of that particular cross to flower. This is something of a coup, like winning a horse race. Because of this Mr. Black graciously named the cypripedium Jacqueline Kranz.

You can also propagate orchids from back bulbs. These are the bulbs that have already flowered which are attached to the back of a growing plant. Whether you wish to propagate them or not, they should be removed so as not to interfere with the vigor of the parent plant. The bulbs are planted in an orchid-growing medium and given an 18-hour day under a high light intensity. Leaves appear—and you have a new orchid plant started. It sounds much easier than growing them from seed, but usually the plants are slow in developing, and the results are rarely as good as with orchids grown from seed.

However you assemble your collection, whether it comprises only a few plants or enough to fill your entire greenhouse, you will find that this is no overstatement: growing orchids is a fascinating experience.

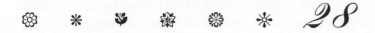

28

AFRICAN VIOLETS

African violets (*Saintpaulia*) have the distinction of being among the first plants to make a debut under artificial lights in the home. Probably no plant is more popular. Its leaves are exchanged today with the same zeal with which plant-lovers of yesteryear exchanged begonia slips. One reason for their popularity is that even under a relatively small amount of artificial light they blossom, and with 600 to 1000 foot-candles they are some of the most delightful plants an amateur can grow.

Only under the constancy of artificial lighting have they become "easy" flowering plants. In fact, it took us more than a year to penetrate the secret as to why some blossomed profusely and some didn't. We grew rows and rows of them under different lights, in different temperatures, in different soils. Finally, the day came when there were literally dozens upon dozens of single and double blossoms—pink, white, blue, purple. We viewed them with the pride of a student who has solved a difficult problem in calculus. We could now take a leaf from any blossoming plant and know, with the assurance that comes from demonstration, that five months later we would have another blossoming plant. And you can do it too. There are some problems that beset the uninitiated, but there are also short-cuts which will give you a blossoming plant in record time.

Because so many wish to grow the African violet, its propagation from a leaf is discussed in considerable detail. You will find, by following these instructions, that it is a simple matter to grow a clean, beautifully flowering plant, provided you take advantage of artificial lights.

❋ *Propagating the African Violet*

Cut the leaf from the variety you wish to grow, using a good sharp knife and leaving a stem about 2 to 2½ inches long. Choose a vigorously growing leaf from a healthy plant, not a mature one that has lost its bright color. It is important to select a leaf from a healthy plant because leaves from retarded plants are often slow in developing roots.

Immediately after cutting the leaf is the time to rout the cyclamen mite or any other pests that may happen to be inconspicuously present. Give them a bath, along with the leaf, in Aramite. Allow the substance to dry on the leaf surface. The next morning, wash it off thoroughly in a stream of running water. As a double check, repeat the performance a few days later. This treatment means you should have clear sailing from here on in as far as pests are concerned. Between treatments you will, of course, keep the leaf in water.

Put two or three leaves together in water in the same propagating bottle, so they will support each other in a horizontal position, thereby getting the full benefit of the light. African violets often take months to root on the windowsill, but under artificial lights a healthy leaf roots in three weeks. The length of time it takes a leaf to root is repeated in the growing cycle of the tiny plantlets that will form on it. Thus, it will take the same length of time for the new plantlet to develop as it does for the leaf to form roots.

When a few roots, ⅛ to ¼ inch in length, have formed on the leaf, it should be planted in soil in a 2¼-inch pot. The tip of the stem, where the roots form, should be at least 1 to 1½ inches beneath the surface of the soil; this will give a fairly long section for root development of the new plantlets as they push upward through the soil.

The soil must be kept moist at all times while the plantlets are growing. The wick, or self-watering, method pays big dividends here.

When the plantlets have developed two or three leaves each, they can usually be safely transplanted to their individual pots. The easiest way to tell whether the plantlets are ready or not is to take the ball of earth out of the old pot and pull the dirt away until you can examine the roots. If the plants are well rooted, separate them from the parent leaf and plant them. Any that are not well rooted should be left on the parent and replanted with it; it will not be long before they develop sturdy roots too. In setting out the new plantlets, you should bury the roots as deeply as you did the stem of the parent leaf from which they grew.

African violets are generally prolific. The same leaf is capable of producing several groups of new plants. We planted a single Bluebird leaf seven times, and it gave us a total of forty-nine children in a short space of time. The last set was just as vigorous as the first, and had we given the leaf a chance, it would have produced more plants.

After a leaf has produced a set of plantlets, many growers cut all its roots, believing it necessary to root the leaf again before it will produce more progeny. This "profiteth nothing," nor is it good policy, for the quality of the plants is not improved by this time-consuming process.

Many African violets send out flower buds by the time they have from seven to ten leaves. They also seek to propagate by producing a multiplicity of crowns, which first appear on a plant as two tiny leaves attached to the main stem at the leaf axil. While they are small, these crowns can be broken off with the point of a pencil or a small knife without injury to the main part of the stem or to the big leaf. As the crowns become larger, it is more difficult to remove them without injuring the plant. But if the crowns are not removed they delay the plant in its flowering for a long, long time.

Sometimes you may wish to keep two or three crowns on a plant; in so doing, you are growing two or three plants on the same root. Thus, eventually, you get a larger plant with more blossoms. Take care in deciding which crowns you will allow to develop. Your aim is to keep those that will give you the best-balanced and most symmetrical plant. Continue to remove all the other new crowns, just as you would in growing a single-crown plant.

Usually the varieties that flower soonest are those that develop the most numerous crowns. The tendency exists, however, in all varieties. More crowns appear in young plants, but even old ones produce them.

Sometimes it is hard to distinguish a flower bud from a small crown. In many varieties, the bud seems to be covered by a small leaf on either side. However, until you get experience in distinguishing between the two, it is wise to leave the new growth for a short period of time. By looking closely you can usually recognize a flower bud when the stem is ¼ inch long.

All the cultural directions given in this book apply especially to growing the African violet. In addition, their needs are briefly summarized in the following paragraphs. These will help you to know exactly how to grow these beautiful saintpaulias under artificial light, as well as enable you to put your finger on what keeps your old plant from blooming.

❀ *Needs of African Violets*

Light. African violets can be grown under either fluorescent or filament lamps. They grow better under fluorescent, but they grow best under the proper combination of the two. Balanced lighting increases the number of buds and blossoms on a plant by more than 50 per cent. The length of time that the flowers last is also greatly influenced by the type of light used; under fluorescent tubes, blossoms remain on the stems for an average of from three to six days; under balanced lighting, the blossoms remain for three weeks.

Profusion of bloom is also increased by giving them a cycle of 18 hours of lamplight a day. They flower, however, when given less. To check this, we grew large numbers of plants for considerable periods in a variety of cycles. African violets, we found, will flower in a cycle of only 12 or 13 hours of lamplight, beneath a light intensity of 250 to 350 foot-candles. Under these conditions the flowering is sparse; we never had more than a half-dozen flowers open on a plant at one time. Some varieties would have two or three blossoms open with only 100 foot-candles of light. When the light intensity was increased to between 350 and 400 foot-candles, there were twice as many blossoms in the 12-hour light cycle, and many more in the 16- to 18-hour cycle.

However, when the light cycle was lengthened to 16 to 18 hours of lamplight with a light intensity of 600 to 1000 foot-candles, two things were most noticeable. The plant grew very rapidly and many more flowers opened; also, because the growing conditions were so improved, the flowers lasted twice as long. This was particularly true of the single violets. As for the doubles, one sent out three flower stems from one leaf axil.

Leaves stretching upward on long stems indicate that the plants do not have quite enough light; when the stems are short and the leaves bend downward over the pot, there is too much light; when the leaves of African violets lie chiefly in a horizontal plane with only a few pointing upward, the light intensity just suits their needs.

Temperature. African violets are at their best in a temperature between 68 and 70 degrees Fahrenheit; but they will grow in a temperature that ranges from 60 to 85 degrees. In high temperatures the flowers are small and do not last as well. Though saintpaulias endure heat, they will die if the temperature is cold. At 50 degrees or lower, crown rot starts, the leaves begin to wilt, and the flowers will drop off.

Soil. After growing African violets in hundreds of different soil mixtures, we can say with conviction that they are *very sensitive* to the slightest changes. They will grow better in the soil mixture given here than in the innumerable others we tried; in fact, they grow so well you can almost see the leaves unfold.

Since it is practically impossible to remove old soil from the thickly matted roots of mature plants, transplanting them into this recommended soil is only a partial cure. Therefore, the safest and quickest method is to grow new plants from the leaves of any old African violets that you cherish. These new plantlets can then be given the benefit of a soil mixture they like.

It is necessary to examine the manner of growth of the roots of your plants. If the soil is compatible, the roots completely penetrate it, growing straight out to the sides of the pot from the center. In soil that is not quite suited to them, they grow near the surface and down the sides of the pots. In very poor soil, the roots are close to the top, rarely reaching the bottom of the pot.

Fertilizer. Fertilizing African violets is most important. They need the right amount of food to blossom abundantly. Too much or too little results in sparseness of bloom. We water our African violets every two weeks with the fertilizing mixture recommended in Chapter 18.

Occasionally, even this amount will suddenly cause a plant to stop growing. It is best to test the soil for nitrates if this happens. Also, look at the root growth. It will tell how successfully you are meeting the plant's food needs. A good root system indicates that all is well. A tiny root system at the top of the pot may well indicate too rich a soil. It definitely points out that the plant and the soil are incompatible.

Watering. Under artificial lights, watering African violets is not the problem it is on the windowsill. There, it is often essential to water them from the bottom, by pouring water into their saucers and pouring it off twenty minutes later. Sunlight striking a leaf which holds a small drop of water causes an unsightly brown spot. You can safely water them in a normal manner under artificial lights, for, as long as you use lukewarm water, brown spots will not appear on the leaves. Keeping the soil moist at all times, however, ensures more profuse blooming.

Pots. African violets are more frequently overpotted than underpotted. This is the chronology you should use: Tiny plantlets from the parent leaf go into 2¼-inch pots. There they should remain—you know the rule we've given—"until their roots completely penetrate the ball of earth." This usually takes from three to six months, at which time the plant should be in blossom.

From this pot they are stepped up only one size—to 2½-inch pots— worth repeating, too, for you will scarcely believe a pot of that size is large enough for such a well-rooted plant. Leaves grow so much faster than roots that you can safely keep it in this size until it has a leaf spread of from 8 to 10 inches. When it has reached this size, it is ready for a 3-inch pot, where most violets are content to spend their days. You may possibly grow a few big plants which need slightly larger pots.

Transplanting. Transplanting African violets from one pot to another is difficult for most amateurs because these plants have very thickly matted roots and exceptionally tender, brittle leaves. It once seemed to us an almost impossible task to move one of these plants to a larger pot without spoiling the symmetry of its leaf growth. We seemed always to end up with plants that had leaves on one side and not on the other, as though mischievous parakeets had pecked them off.

To help those of us who are not deft-fingered, we devised a novel but most effective way of transplanting. Instead of putting some soil in the bottom of the larger pot, setting the plant in it, and packing earth around its roots and the accompanying ball of earth, you prepare in the pot what looks like a dirt nest. With your fingers, press the soil against the sides and bottom so you have a cavity just large enough to fit the ball of earth. Those with a good eye may get the hole exactly right the first time. Others may have to make two or three attempts. If the hole is too big or too little, fill the pot with earth and try again. This method is certainly not according to Hoyle, but if you use it your plant will come through the transfer with all its leaves, and will soon be happily adjusted to its new home.

Dealing with the Cyclamen Mite. One of the first indications that a cyclamen mite infests a plant is a change in the color of the leaves, close to the base, where they spring from the stem. Here the leaves will look markedly lighter in color and will appear to be wet. You will be able to notice the difference in color even at the bases of the leaves that are normally bicolored. If leaves so attacked grow at all, they will be misshapen in outline.

As the infestation becomes greater, there is a second stage. The leaves in the center of the plant bunch together and do not seem to grow. Their color continues to be light, but some of the leaves will begin to shrivel. Growth is finally halted entirely, for the plant can no longer obtain nourishment through its leaves.

In the third stage, the small leaves turn brownish. Examine them with a magnifying glass and you will see that the tiny leaf hairs are short, curled up, and brownish.

In the fourth stage, the entire top of the crown becomes smooth and brown. Only minute brown stumps of the leaf stems remain.

Oftentimes a plant which is a victim of the cyclamen mite will have deformed blossoms. The pest may have been held under control sufficiently for the flower buds to develop, but when they open, one or two petals may be missing; or they may be misshapen; or only the stamens develop, with no surrounding petals. You can be sure there are cyclamen mites on the plant if the flower stems loop or twist. Sometimes one will make a complete circle.

🏵 *Varieties*

It would take a brave man to tell you what kind of African violets you should grow. All are beautiful, whether they be blue or pink or lavender; double or single; or how they may be named. We still love and grow the old variety Pink Lady, because it won a first prize for us at the International Flower Show. Its great-great-great-and-so-on grandchildren still look to us like prize-winners. There are hundreds of named varieties which will grow so luxuriantly under artificial lights that you can take your pick and grow what you will.

We have found it better to buy from local growers. Then you can see for yourself how the plants flower, the size of the blooms, and especially whether the plants are healthy and free from pests. You will be surprised to find that most growers cultivate relatively few varieties—those that have been proved by trial and error. Generally these are the popular varieties that propagate easily, grow rapidly, and flower profusely. These are the qualities to look for in African violets.

African violets vary in many ways, not only in the shape, surface, and coloring of their leaves, but in the rapidity of their growth, the size and color of their flowers, the number on a stem, and the length of time their blossoms last.

We find that under artificial lights the double African violets make most outstanding plants. Because their blossoms are so long-lasting, often remaining in good condition for three weeks or more, they give an effect of rare abundance. They are hardy, too. The doubles are always the ones that survive the blasts of cold air that strike them when we linger late into the fall at our camp in the woods. Others often languish and die. They are also less susceptible to unconsumed gas fumes than are most singles. As if these virtues were not enough, they have the added advantage of being especially easy to propagate.

What you grow is up to you, but whatever you choose, remember this simple maxim: Grow it from a leaf.

GESNERIADS

Had it not been for African violets, gardeners under lights might have missed an entire genus of beautiful flowers, the gesneriads. There are over two thousand original species and a host of beautiful flowering hybrids. Like the orchids, few gesneriads have popular names, but once you are familiar with the botanical ones, they roll off your tongue as easily as gloxinia.

As gardeners discover how beautifully these showy flowers grow under lights, they become favorites. It was a gesneriad, the *Tula flava*, that won for us a purple ribbon at the International Flower Show. And all of its cousins, sisters, and brothers have grown with the same grace. They prove their worth under a light intensity of from 1000 to 1500 foot-candles, but there are many that will grow and flower, though not as abundantly, at a light intensity of 750 to 1000.

If you have four Power-Groove tubes and incandescent lamps, shielded, you can grow practically any of the gesneriads. They have a common love for humidity and light. They need a well-drained soil that must not dry out. We recommend automatic watering; put a wick in every pot and let it extend to the galvanized pan below. This will keep the gesneriads watered and the water will also make the humidity high in your greenhouse case.

❃ *Gloxinias*

Solomon in all his glory could not equal the splendor of the blossoming gloxinia. The large, tubular flowers in their royal robes of red and purple, or varied as the sunset, are among the loveliest of blossoms. Through the miracle of artificial light, they will blossom not only in the summer but all the year through. Gloxinias are much easier to grow than poinsettias, and a red one at Christmastime makes an even more glowing display.

Gloxinias are light-sensitive seeds. Until this fact was known, the tubers were hard to grow from seed. Seeds germinate best at a temperature of 65 degrees Fahrenheit, and usually need a 15-day exposure to light to germinate. They should be transplanted immediately to 2½-inch pots. They need to be fertilized much oftener than most seedlings because they like nitrates, but don't overdo it or you will have stunted plants. If you do not wish to grow them from seed, tubers of this plant can be purchased from any number of reliable dealers. Plant the tubers in soil and place them under lights. Some break their dormancy earlier than others, and you should try to pick those that show signs of life. These will blossom first, in about six months, and by planting them at two- or three-week intervals, you will have a succession of blooms out of doors. Indoors, if well treated, they blossom every month of the year.

You can also grow a tuber from a leaf. Follow the same procedure you use with African violets. The tuber that forms on the parent leaf may not send up leaves, however, for more than six months.

The secret of success with gloxinias is to give them plenty of food. We know a successful grower who waters them once a day with a dilute solution of fertilizer. We compromise and water them with our fertilizer solution twice a week after the plant is in full growth. Gloxinias are so large and grow so rapidly that they need much extra nourishment.

The buds open rapidly and last a long time. With the right amount of light and the proper amount of fertilizer, a gloxinia that was started from a good tuber should grow into a plant with fifteen or twenty flowers open at one time, and more ready to develop.

You should give the gloxinia 600 foot-candles of light. It will grow and blossom with only 450 or 500 foot-candles, but its leaves will point upward instead of back over the sides of the pot. With the lower light intensity, the stems of the flowers will be elongated and rather weak.

While the plants are growing they must be kept moist. After their blossoming period you can take them out of the light and allow the tubers to become dormant. Remove the tubers from the dirt and store them at about 45 to 50 degrees Fahrenheit. You can use them over and over again if you give them rest periods.

The amount of rest needed by a tuber varies. One that has been well fed and cared for during its growing period will probably show signs of new life within five to six months, and sometimes less. Two and a half to three months after the tuber is again planted in soil, the flowers should appear. However, if you manage to have the light just to their liking they seem to get along without resting and become ever-blooming under lights. But they must be well fertilized and never allowed to dry out.

Because gloxinias need all the light you can give them, you should plan on 18 hours of lamplight and 6 of darkness. They have flowered for us, however, with their tops close to a three-tubed fluorescent light and two incandescent bulbs, under only 13 hours of lamplight. They blossomed well, but their stems were weak and elongated.

Perhaps you will find (though we hope not) that as the buds come out they turn brown. If so, nothing can be done about it, for this is the sign of the cyclamen mite. To avoid this kind of disappointment, keep your plants clean, and always, before planting the tubers, give them a dipping in Malathion, or take the time to grow your gloxinias from seed.

❀ *Achimenes*

Achimenes have been grown in England since 1778, but they waned in popularity at the beginning of this century. Thanks to their great beauty under lights, they are again finding enthusiastic supporters here. They are also being grown for summer gardens, but they grow better indoors under lights. Many of them are hanging plants. If you have tiers of three lights, you can grow some of them on the top tier and they give a look of great abundance to your collection. To a degree this is true of most of the hanging gesneriads. (Notice the hanging plant that is being grown under a Gro-Lux lamp in the photograph section following p. 52; it is not an achimenes, however, but an episcia.) What makes the achimenes so delightful is that the flowers grow from axils of the leaves. In a well-flowered plant the large beautiful flowers against the leafy background are unique. There are many flower colors from which to choose: red, yellow, orange, blue-violet, and white. The plants have been hybridized and you can buy the rhizomes from which they grow, or you can buy some good seeds and have any number from which to choose. If you prefer the named varieties, some hybrids developed by Cornell University are excellent. And then there is Purple King, one of the most popular achimenes in the United States. This is based on its garden performance. Under lights its masses of flowers stop the show.

❀ Other Varieties

Columneas, also gesneriads, do well under lights. Of the many we grew, the one that stands out in memory is *Columnea microphylla.* There was something about its fine-textured foliage and numerous blossoms that gave it the appeal of the miniature. Actually the plant itself is quite large, but everything about it is delicate.

Most gardeners think of the episcas as needing a terrarium setting to do well. We always object if anyone suggests that any of our indoor greenhouses are terrariums, but we gracefully accepted the implication when it came from the episcias. They outdid themselves. They need moist soil, a humid atmosphere, and a light intensity of between 750 and 1000 foot-candles. With these requirements filled they are extremely beautiful.

The streptocarpus grows well under the same conditions. There is a lovely species from South Africa which grew for us for several years until we lost it when we took it to camp one summer. *Streptocarpus vandeleuri* has beautiful ivory-white flowers with yellow-green markings on their throats, all crowded together on stems fully a foot in length.

BEGONIAS

The begonia ranks second only to the African violet in its value to the lamplight gardener. In fact, when we discovered the soil begonias liked, the light intensity they needed, and how to grow certain varieties, we almost felt that begonias ranked first. Fortunately it is not necessary to choose; you can grow both violets and begonias under the same installation of lights and achieve the variety one does out of doors by using different flowers.

Begonias, however, are not as tolerant of low light intensities as African violets. To become an enthusiastic grower of begonias you need to have a light intensity of at least 1000 foot-candles. They become superb plants in a light intensity of 1000 to 1500 foot-candles, and with Power-Groove tubes this is within easy reach of the amateur. Some semperflorens, metallica, and rex can be grown at 600 foot-candles, but they too do better with more light.

We have grown at least forty different varieties of begonias in our lamplight greenhouse—more, in fact, if the various types of semperflorens were included in this count. Some varieties never flowered for us; others flowered but sparsely. All are individualists, as we discovered when we grew one hundred nineteen semperflorens begonias from seeds; no two were alike.

Of course, their fundamental chracteristics were very similar. Each had the same attractive small, shiny, green leaves, and each bore the same type of flowers. But they differed greatly in size, in ability to flower under lights, in the duration of their flowers, and in color. Their flowers ranged from white to carmine red, with intermediate shades of light pink, medium pink, and rose.

We had hoped to find among them one that equaled the semperflorens which Grandmother gave us as a slip the first year we were married. Year after year it really earned its title of "ever-blooming." In the spring we would set it out in a sheltered spot in the garden, where it was always covered with blooms. In late summer, we would cut off branches to make new slips. These would begin blossoming as soon as they were rooted. In the darkest days of winter this begonia blossomed on our windowsill as well as it did in early spring. Those were the almost-forgotten days of maids, but I still remember how Sally used to complain about those blossoms. "My lawse," she would say, "this begonia's worse than a canary. I sweep up its worn-out blossoms every day, and the next day it just has a new lot for me to sweep. Makes you hate to look at its pink blossoms. You know you'll be sweeping 'em."

But, sadly enough, none of the others even approached in "ever-blooming" that plant of Grandmother's. They did well enough under artificial lights, but as soon as we tried a promising aspirant on the windowsill the blossoms disappeared. We found we did better with "named" varieties of the semperflorens. These have been specially selected for their free-flowering habits and, to some extent, for their foliage.

You will find that any single-flowered semperflorens, named or unnamed, will easily blossom under a light intensity between 450 and 600 foot-candles. But just as African-violet growers pass by the early favorite Blue Boy, constant bloomer that it is, so we have passed by the single-flowered semperflorens for others that are more spectacular.

The double-flowered semperflorens grow as easily as the single variety, and are more interesting. They produce from six to eight buds on a stem, and the buds remind you of tiny roses. There is a strain known as the New Hampshire hybrids that grow very well in a lamplight garden. The one we had began to blossom when it was scarcely two inches tall, and it continued to produce its beautiful double flowers all winter, and all summer too. It blossoms well with a relatively low light intensity of 350 to 600 foot-candles.

The calla begonia is another form of the semperflorens we had never been able to grow until we grew it by lamplight. Its variegated green and white leaves are so placed as to give the actual impression of tiny, ethereal calla lilies.

The dark, bronzy-leafed varieties of the semperflorens begonia are also interesting. These darker-leafed types need somewhat more light to blossom well.

But variable as the semperflorens may be, the Christmas begonia stands out, to us, as the one that did not come true to form, for one of our plants proved to be as free-flowering as even Grandmother's famous semperflorens, and many times lovelier.

Christmas begonias are hybrids. Several have succeeded the original Gloire de Lorraine, of *Begonia socotrana*, which was once rated the finest hybrid ever grown. The Christmas begonia usually grows only beautiful green leaves during the long days of spring and summer, and does not begin to flower until the days become shorter.

This was where our plant differed. It flowered under 18 hours of 1500 foot-candles of light in our lamplight greenhouse as beautifully as it did under 10 hours of light. Moreover, it flowered just as prolifically on a windowsill in July as in our lamplight greenhouse in December, and its many progeny have continued to behave in the same manner. Sometimes a single blossom will remain open for five or six weeks before the petals drop off.

Your Christmas begonia may not behave like this special one of ours, but it will give you great enjoyment if you make cuttings and grow them under lights.

Give your plants 10 hours of lamplight, and you will find that they too will blossom when they reach a height of two inches, and keep right on blossoming. In a case devoted to short-day plants they will be some of the loveliest flowers in your winter garden.

Many begonias—and all of the rhizomatous types we have grown—need a short day to blossom well. The star begonia, *B. heracleifolia*, needs a 10-hour day for about 6 to 8 weeks to set buds. After the buds are set, the length of day does not seem to matter. When we were growing a star begonia in our long-day case, we tried in vain to remember to take it out each day, after 10 hours of light, and give it darkness under a pail, and we finally gave up. Some may be able to grow short-day plants and long-day plants together by carefully manipulating them, but we can't. We finally put it on the windowsill, which was a fortunate decision, for there it was a beautiful winter show-off. You too will enjoy the picture made by its star-shaped leaves outlined against the frosted pane. Seven lobes form the leaves, which are a deep green, splashed with a lighter green and silver at the veins, underlined with scarlet. When the late-afternoon sun shines through the leaves, you get a delightful effect of brilliant red, green, and silver. The long, succulent hairs that cover the stems add to this play of light and shade.

After it has brightened the living room for six or eight weeks, we take the plant back to our indoor greenhouse, for though the flowers will develop on the windowsill, they are much more prolific under lamplight.

The begonias that have given us the most spectacular amount of bloom, however, are of the strain known as Danish hybrids. These are among newly developed begonias that are making history in the flower world. You can scarcely describe them without feeling like a seed-catalog enthusiast describing a "new sensation." The leaves are a large-sized edition of those of the Christmas begonia, and our plants have salmon-pink flowers that remind you of tuberous-rooted varieties.

Under a light intensity of 450 foot-candles and a cycle of 18 hours, this Danish hybrid grows completely normally, sending up, in about four months' time, from three to six flower spikes. On one of these we counted twenty-six flowers. As these are double and more than two inches across, you can see why it steals the show in any indoor greenhouse.

You can move it to your living room, where it will grow for about a month, especially if it spends part of the time there under a fluorescent light. After this excursion it will need to be rejuvenated under balanced lighting.

Begonia haageana, also called *B. scharffi*, is a short-day plant. We would scarcely call this begonia one of our greatest successes, but it was definitely not a failure. It, too, is picturesque on a windowsill, for as the winter sun shines through its olive-green leaves lined with orange-red, they seem almost transparent. However, this begonia is famed for its blossoms, and we have not yet succeeded in having it produce its large sprays of beautiful flowers. Perhaps it needs a still shorter day. We are listing it, temporarily, for its foliage, and are working hard on the secrets that will make it flower in our lamplight garden.

The lucerna begonia really comes into its own under artificial lights. Under a combination of filament and fluorescent lamps, its leaves grow to a length of almost twelve inches and its flower trusses are larger than those of any begonia we have ever seen. A strong stem grows out from the leaf axil and continues to divide almost endlessly. On the stem appear, at first, heart-shaped stamened flowers, deep pink to bright red in color. These seldom open, but when they begin to drop off the stem divides further and produces long, pendulous, pistillate flowers, nearly three-quarters of an inch across and fully two inches in length. These hang on for a period of two or three weeks. It is not at all unusual to have fifty to sixty of these flowers in a single cluster. When one cluster disappears, others appear farther along the stem.

The plant has a tendency to grow tall, and should be pinched back so that three or four branches develop along the main stem. Likewise, when you propagate it, you should use a short cutting. (It will root in two or three weeks.) Plant it so that the upper leaf is just above the surface of the soil. As soon as two or three leaves develop, pinch off the tip of the stem. The lucerna needs to be watered regularly with a fertilizer solution. It grows well under the same light intensity as the Danish hybrids.

We had to give one of our lucernas away because it grew so bumptiously. A 4-inch cutting grew 2 feet and developed 6 flower stems that were so heavy with flowers that we had to tie them up—and all this in only four months' time! It was the most beautiful background plant we have ever had in our greenhouse, but it quite outgrew its quarters.

We gave it to a schoolteacher friend, who placed it in a south window where it was shielded from the direct rays of the sun by an over-hanging roof. The lucerna immediately demonstrated that it would also grow in a window, if the window were to its liking. When our friend left for the holidays, she instructed her janitor to keep the plant watered; but he forgot, and upon her return she found a prostrate lucerna. Its vigor quickly revived, however, after one good soaking—even to the flower stems—so great was the vitality of the plant.

The Arthur Mallot begonia is distinctive and does not have the six-foot aspirations of the lucerna. It develops flower bracts quite similar to lucerna, but they are smaller, on a scale becoming to the size of the plant. The pistillate flowers are especially lovely, being two-toned, deep and light pink. It has exceptionally beautiful foliage. The leaves are dark red, pointed, and notched. They gradually become darker and glossier, and seem, under lamplight, to have an almost metallic sheen. Arthur Mallots are excellent companions for the Danish hybrids and the lucerna.

The maple-leafed begonia, *B. weltoniensis*, has maplelike leaves and an abundance of blossoms. Both the white-flowered and the pink-flowered ones are excellently suited to lamplight gardening. Their delicate leaves and branching habits add a distinctive accent to your lamplight garden.

But one of the loveliest of them all is the tuberous-rooted begonia of our summer gardens, *B. tuberhybrida*, of the multiflora type. We do not grow this from seeds, but from cuttings made from our tuberous-rooted begonias when they are still at the peak of their beauty. These cuttings may be rooted in water, under lights; or, if you have built an outdoor propagating frame, as described earlier, they may be rooted there in vermiculite. When rooted they are planted in pots and given a 16- to 18-hour day under lights. They will keep on blooming the winter through.

From these same begonias you can also get a second garden dividend, by rooting cuttings from them in the winter or early spring and growing them under lights until they are ready to be set out of doors in June. They will be far showier and have many more flowers than the begonia grown from tubers.

✿ ✳ ❦ ✾ ❀ ✳ *31*

OTHER OUTSTANDING

FLOWERS

If you have a light intensity of 650 foot-candles in your indoor green-house, a large number of plants will flower for you. As the light intensity is increased to 1000, 1200, and 1500 foot-candles, you are rewarded with flowers, more flowers, and still more flowers, as long as the ratio of at least 1 watt of incandescent to every 3 watts of fluorescent is maintained.

To grow any type of flower, you will need at least two areas of light: one where you can grow plants that like a short day and need a temperature around 50 degrees Fahrenheit to form buds, and another set for plants that like a long day and a night temperature around 65 degrees. But you can grow so many beautiful plants with a light intensity of from 1000 to 1500 foot-candles and a temperature between 65 and 75 degrees that many home gardeners settle for a single case. That is a temperature easy to achieve in a house or apartment if you have a duct to a window for control, and are using eight, or even four to six Power-Groove tubes with incandescent lamps. It gives you sufficient light intensity to grow what have always been considered "florist plants."

✸ *Cinerarias*

Sometimes, under lamplight, a plant comes out of character, and experienced florists shake their heads and declare that they never heard of such a thing. This happened with one of our cinerarias. Normally the cineraria needs a period of six weeks of short days and temperatures about 50 degrees Fahrenheit to set buds, after which it can be given a long day. In glass-covered greenhouses cinerarias send up crowns of flowers in early spring. Under lights the flower buds appear and start to grow as soon as the day is lengthened.

But this particular cineraria charted a course of its own. We brought home a tiny seedling with only two leaves, one of which had frozen on the way home. With some misgivings we placed it in our 4-by-6-foot lamplight greenhouse, where the light intensity was about 650 foot-candles.

Accustomed as we were to the rapid growth of plants under artificial lights, the cineraria made us marvel. When it had five leaves it sent up a flower bud. Then more flower stems appeared. At the end of six weeks it had seven full-grown leaves and twenty-two wide-open blossoms. When these were cut off, new buds began to form, and there was another whirl of flowers. This process was repeated several times. It started to bloom three weeks before Christmas, and continued until four weeks before Easter. All the time it was grown in a temperature of 65 degrees with 16 hours of lamplight and 8 hours of darkness. Its actions were all the more surprising, considering that in the summer in the garden it simply grows leaves. Subjecting it to a period of 40 degrees after the seedlings have a few leaves has proved successful. Certainly the cineraria merits more study.

You will enjoy growing it, however it behaves for you, because in the light intensities that you can easily obtain indoors you can be certain of blossoms. By planting the seeds at intervals of every four weeks you can have beautiful blooming plants for a large part of the winter. They can be grown easily from seed, and they come in a great variety of colors. You will find them among the most satisfactory of ornamental plants for growing under lights.

❀ *Poinsettias*

The poinsettia too can be successfully flowered under artificial lights, but you must have a knowledge of its habits. Slips taken from a Christmas plant root quickly. Under lights poinsettia stems quickly turn woody, and the slips should be taken from green wood.

The young plants grow rapidly in an indoor greenhouse where the light intensity is somewhat over 500 foot-candles and the temperature above 60 degrees Fahrenheit. As soon as our new plants are well-branched and husky, and between 12 and 15 inches tall, we shorten their day by giving them 9 hours of lamplight and 15 of darkness. They must be kept extremely moist during this period. Their roots should never dry out, and certainly not when the buds are forming. It is extremely important that during their "night" absolutely no light reaches them. If it does, the buds do not form.

At the end of eight weeks, the plants usually begin to show tiny buds. If the temperature rises to more than 65 degrees while the buds are forming, they will not open, so you must watch the temperature carefully at this time.

Of course this treatment does not give you poinsettias at the Christmas season. To have poinsettias at Christmas takes still more manipulating. The plants are allowed to grow in your greenhouse with a long day until summer, when they are sunk in pots in the garden. We do not bring these plants into our indoor greenhouse in the fall, for they would be too tall to place under our lights. Instead, we slip them again, and grow new plants which fit under the lights and can be made to flower at Christmas.

Poinsettia leaves drop off if they are left in a draft. While you are growing them in your lamplight greenhouse you will have no trouble, but warn the friends to whom you give them to keep them out of cold breezes.

❀ *Cyclamens*

Cyclamens are among the most beautiful plants that can be brought to flower in your indoor greenhouse, but to grow them successfully takes at least a year's foresight and constant vigilance to keep them free from pests. The cyclamen, you must remember, gave the destructive cyclamen mite its name. If you don't watch out, there is always danger that it may find your plants, deform the flowers, cause them to be peculiarly streaked with deeper shades of color, or keep them from blossoming altogether.

The only safe method is to grow plants from seed. Seeds can be purchased in packages of one hundred and, since they are sold in assorted colors, you can have a beautiful display. The cyclamen grows true to form and color from seed, so, if you prefer, you may buy named varieties.

As cyclamens form tubers before they send up any leaves, the method of germinating and growing them is modified from the one used in propagating most seedlings. (See Chapter 22, "Seed-Sowing.") The 4-inch seed pan is prepared as directed and filled by putting in ½ inch of coarse vermiculite, 1½ inches of the regular potting soil, and over this ⅛ to ¼ inch of finer vermiculite. It is then well moistened, and the seeds are placed about ½ inch apart on top of the last layer of vermiculite; to ensure constant moisture, the pot is covered with a piece of glass; if the soil appears too moist, the glass should be pushed aside until the surface appears just damp. The pot is kept in a pan in which the depth of water is constantly maintained between ¼ and ⅜ of an inch.

It is usually from eight to ten weeks before any surface growth appears. When the first leaf projects above the surface, carefully transplant into a 2¼-inch pot. The tuber will have very few roots. For good root growth it is important that the soil be constantly, uniformly moist, so use a wick in this small pot, or some other form of automatic watering. Cyclamen seeds rarely germinate all at one time. We have had them come up at different intervals over a two-month period.

Vigilance against the cyclamen mite must begin as soon as the leaves are out of the ground. Do not germinate the plants where you are growing African violets, and keep the young plantlets away from them and any other plants which might be hosts to the mite. If you have a goodly number of plants it is safest to grow them under a special set of lights. They do not need balanced lighting at this time, so they can be grown under only a few fluorescent tubes, provided these are only a few inches above the plants. Give them an 18-hour day, if possible, during the growing period, for the greater the light intensity, the faster they develop. As soon as the plants are large enough and the roots have well penetrated the soil, shift them into 3-inch pots. As they grow, they must be transferred to still larger pots. The great majority will take 5-inch pots, but some may grow large enough to require 6-inch pots.

It is safer to keep cyclamens in the house during the summer months, although we have summered them on benches in the woods most successfully. When grown out of doors, they must be kept away from the delphinium and the monkshood, which sometimes harbor the cyclamen mite. Be equally careful not to bring spikes of these beautiful flowers into the house if your cyclamens are growing there under lights. Indoors or out, continue to use automatic watering to keep the roots moist. Beautiful and abundant blooming depends upon this. Some of the large plants may take a quart of water a day while they blossom.

Cyclamens can be grown to blossom at Christmas by planting the seeds in November or earlier during the previous year. Seeds planted in late August or early September give larger plants. Whenever they are planted, they can be grown under fluorescent tubes alone for a year; after that they need balanced lighting and a short day. They also like to grow in a cool greenhouse.

For eight to ten weeks we give cyclamens a night temperature of 50 to 55 degrees Fahrenheit, combined with a light cycle of 10 hours of lamplight and 14 hours of darkness. During this period the buds form and the growth is vigorous. As soon as the buds appear, the light is increased to 16 hours of lamplight and 8 hours of darkness.

The blossoms are luxuriant, beautiful, and long-lasting. The ruffled varieties are especially appealing. You can use one or two of them for a corsage and feel as if you were wearing orchids.

Fuchsias

Fuchsias, with their long, tubular flowers, are familiar to gardeners, who have grown them in many countries down through the years. A story often told in horticultural circles illustrates the grace of not being too sure of oneself: For more than a century and a half, a controversy waged over a species of fuchsia described by the great botanist Linnaeus as having only four stamens. He based his description on a drawing that had been made in 1730 by Plummer, by whom the species had been imported from the West Indies. The original plant had long since disappeared, and the drawing was considered inaccurate. "Whoever saw or heard of a fuchsia with four stamens?" the horticulturists asked. However, one hundred and seventy years after Plummer had imported his seeds, Thomas Hogg secured some fuchsia seeds from the West Indies. He planted them, and Plummer's fuchsias bloomed again, the exact image of the plant in his "crude drawing."

Fuchsias, since the time of Hogg, have been hybridized, and their forms and colors have become lovelier. There are many beautiful named varieties, which are more satisfactory to grow than those propagated from seed. Wherever it is possible, try to get the named varieties, for they will give you, under artificial lights, flower-laden plants.

Fuchsias like a long cycle of lamplight—18 hours whenever it is possible—but they have another requirement: they must be kept cool at night. If it is possible to give them a temperature of 45 degrees Fahrenheit, you will be rewarded with prolific and continuous bloom. Oftentimes in the home such a low temperature is difficult to attain, and fuchsias will tolerate a night temperature as high as 55 degrees. Daytime temperatures are not important; these may be considerably higher.

Two other practices that also increase the number of flowers are care in keeping the soil moist and frequent fertilizing. Fuchsias are gross feeders and respond perceptibly to extra nutriment.

Unfortunately, they do not have the same immunity to pests as geraniums, for example, so it is imperative to treat any new arrival with insecticide. You must also keep a careful watch to see that they continue to grow as clean plants, for it is a well-grown, clean plant that produces showers of blossoms.

❀ *Freesias*

Freesias too need a cool temperature, if you would have these pendulant, ivory-white flowers bloom for you. They are a special attraction if you install glass shelves at the sides of your indoor greenhouse, where freesias may hang among ivies and ferns, lovely in themselves and breathtaking in their fragrance.

But they must have a short day in order that their buds may form. For six weeks their lamplight sun must rise and set *regularly* in a cycle of 9 hours of lamplight and 15 hours of darkness, in a temperature that is not much higher than 60 degrees Fahrenheit. We speak from experience. We had no trouble in flowering freesias when we were growing them in an indoor greenhouse devoted to short-day plants, but we became so entranced with them that we wanted them in our long-day greenhouse especially when we did not have an area devoted to short-day plants. We intended to take them out every day at four o'clock in the afternoon. Some days, however, in spite of our best efforts, we would forget to take them out from under the lights. Other days we would forget to take them out from under the inverted pail, and they would have 36 hours (or more) of darkness. The plants produced some of the loveliest of green leaves but nary a blossom.

Given a short day consistently, freesias blossom twelve weeks after being planted. The flowers last for a long time unless the temperature gets too warm for them. Then they quickly disappear.

Freesias grow from corms, which form on the top of the previous year's growth. Excellent corms form under artificial lights; these corms can then be planted. If you plant them at three-week intervals you can have a succession of bloom.

✿ *Easter Lilies*

One of the minor yet thrilling joys of lamplight gardening is growing the Easter lily. The flower is beautiful at any time, but the first time you see its white chalice growing under your own lights it seems a special miracle.

We have grown many different flowers, but we still vividly remember opening the door of our closet and seeing the lily in all its beauty, blooming under two small fluorescent tubes. We discovered at that time that the lily would blossom under fluorescent tubes with a light intensity of only 250 foot-candles. We also grew one under a 125-watt tungsten bulb, although the lower leaves yellowed off. However,

the Easter lily achieves a completely normal growth under a light intensity of 450 foot-candles of balanced lighting, with a cycle of 18
hours of lamplight. It prefers a cool temperature, but we have grown
it in our enclosed indoor greenhouse at a temperature of 68 degrees
Fahrenheit. At this temperature the stem is not as strong, nor do the
flowers last as long as when it is grown at a temperature of 55 degrees.

As Easter lily bulbs are usually sold by the hundred instead of by
ones or twos, finding bulbs is difficult for the amateur. Often a florist
will sell you a few from his supply. The Croft Easter lily is the easiest
to handle in the home, for it does not grow tall. Tall-growing varieties
require quite special manipulation of the lights; they must continually
be raised higher.

It takes from three and a half to four months from the time the bulb
is placed in the soil till the flower buds open. With practice you can
make the flowering coincide with Easter, but at first it is wise to con-
centrate on getting the bulb to flower, without regard to the calendar.
A good time to plant it is in the middle of November. The bulb is
placed in a 6-inch pot, level with the soil surface, watered well, and
stored away in a dark place where the temperature is between 55 and
60 degrees Fahrenheit. Like other bulbs, it must be kept moist while it
is hidden away.

Roots develop rapidly. Often in three weeks' time a stem will poke
up through the soil. As soon as this happens, place the bulb under
lights. Throughout the entire growing process the bulb needs fertilizing. Unless it is fed at least once a week it will not develop large,
beautiful flowers.

When the lily has ceased to bloom, it may be planted in the garden,
where, that same summer, it will probably flower a second time. The
Croft Easter lily is a hardy plant and multiplies rapidly.

SPRING-FLOWERING

BULBS

Tulips, hyacinths, squills, crocuses, and daffodils, which indeed "come before the swallow dares," can make your home a veritable spring garden. You need only the simplest accessories to keep spring on your doorstep from mid-January until nature herself is ready to take over.

Lamplight gardening makes it possible for you to force these bulbs with assurance. Those of you who have tried them on the windowsill know the difficulties: the stems of hyacinths are so long and weak that they topple over the side of the pot; tulips blossom at the base of the leaves instead of sending up graceful stems, and daffodils and narcissuses prove so fleeting that it scarcely seems worth the effort to grow them.

Our method of treatment differs somewhat from those used by professional growers, but it is especially adapted to the home and to lamplight gardening. Using it, and the light from only a 100-watt incandescent bulb, you can be certain of success. All of these spring-flowering bulbs will, of course, grow under a fluorescent tube or balanced lighting, but since indoor greenhouses are always crowded, the obliging ways of these spring-flowering bulbs make it possible to save the space for more demanding plants.

Actually, bulbs are kept in the dark a great portion of the time. Like a successful theatrical performance, their brief spell of glory under the lights takes several months of preparation, but it involves little work.

The first step is to purchase the highest-quality bulbs. You will find that most growers offer special bulbs for forcing. They are usually slightly more expensive, but they are well worth the additional cost, for they are large and choice, and therefore produce finer flowers.

The middle of October is the best time to put them into three-quarter pots, as a warm September day may force them prematurely into leaf development. Sort them according to their advancement. In some a tiny yellowish-green sprout will be visible, while in others there will be no sign of life. If you mix the forward with the slow, some will shoot into bloom while others remain curled in their leaves when they are placed under lights.

About one-third of the bulb may protrude above the soil. A 5-inch pot, for example, will hold either four or five tulips, three or four narcissuses, or about twice as many crocuses, squills, or grape hyacinths. Hyacinth bulbs are so much larger that they are often planted alone in a 4-inch pot, or three can be grown together in a 7-inch pot.

As soon as the bulbs are planted, they are watered and put in a dark spot. For this first stage of their development, we have found that a covered box in the garage is an excellent place to store them. The pots must not be piled on top of each other unless they are separated by a layer of straw 12 inches thick. It is preferable to place them in a single layer and cover them with four thicknesses of burlap tucked well down over the edges of the pots. Then the cover of the box is closed. Ideally, they should be kept at a temperature between 35 and 45 degrees Fahrenheit. This can easily be accomplished if you have an outdoor propagating frame. But we did not have an outdoor frame for many years, and can recommend the garage method unconditionally. Actually, the bulbs can freeze and thaw, as long as the process is a gradual one, without being harmed. The protection of the garage, the covered box, and the burlap tucked around the pots was enough so that, even during winters with long periods of zero-degree weather, we never lost a bulb.

Early in the fall the bulbs may need to be watered twice a week, but as soon as the weather grows colder watering them once every two weeks will probably suffice. It is essential that they be kept moist at all times.

Usually by the middle of December some of the hyacinths have developed far enough so they can be brought indoors and started on their way to flowering. Tulips and narcissuses may not be ready until the first of January. You can tell by knocking the ball of earth out of the pots and looking at the roots. The bulbs are ready to be brought indoors when the roots have thoroughly penetrated the soil. Oftentimes the roots will push through the hole in the bottom of the pot.

Occasionally your spring-flowering bulbs will show an unusual zeal to get started. A thick mass of roots will form at the base of the bulb and, instead of penetrating the soil, will push the bulb out to the surface. If the bulbs rise out of place, water thoroughly to soak the soil and patiently force the bulb back into place. This phenomenon is especially common with tulip and narcissus bulbs.

To be certain of a succession of bloom indoors from mid-January to mid-April, bring the pots in at ten-day intervals. Indoors they must be placed in a cool, dark place, with a temperature that is not higher then 55 degrees Fahrenheit. A slightly lower temperature is even better. Since absolute darkness is most important, the safest plan is to invert a pail over the pot. A small amount of light reaching the growing stems changes their yellow color to green and may cause the flower buds to open half an inch or so above the ground.

In January it often takes three weeks for the flower bud to emerge far enough out of the bulb so that it may be placed in the light; in March it takes only ten to twelve days. There is no rule of thumb to tell how much time each pot needs before the flower stem is well out of the bulb so it can be placed under lights. It is best to look at them every few days.

With the tulip, the leaves and flowers are squeezed together so tightly that they appear to be a single stem slightly bulged out at the bottom. This outside leaf looks for all the world like the flame of a candle, with a slight ring where it is attached to the stem. It will be about three-eighths of an inch thick and a full four inches tall before this ring, or bulge, is visible all around the stem. At this point it is ready to be placed under lights.

The hyacinth looks quite different. The leaves and flower stem rise out of the bulb in a tight, compact mass, but as they grow you can, as a rule, easily distinguish the flowers from the leaves. When the leaves are from four to six inches long and the flower buds can be easily seen, place the plant under lights.

Daffodils and narcissuses are kept under the pail in complete darkness somewhat longer. They look like pale, shadowy ghosts, and the flower stem and leaves are both plainly visible. When they are from four to six inches tall, place them under lights.

As soon as any of the bulbs are placed under lights, the leaves quickly become green, and the buds change from yellow to their natural colors. Here, too, it takes longer for the buds to develop into flowers in January than it does in March. With most varieties it takes about the same length of time for the flowers to evolve out of the bulb in the darkness as it takes for them to bloom under the lights.

Tulips will stay in bloom for two weeks if they are kept cool at night. Hyacinths last for eleven or twelve days. Narcissuses are usually in good condition for only four to seven days. Squills, crocuses, and grape hyacinths are quite fleeting; their beauty is gone in four or five days.

Most bulbs, after being forced, can be grown in the garden another year, given a little care. Place them in a cool window and keep them watered till the foliage has turned yellow; then let the soil dry out. After four to six weeks the soil and all the dried portions of the old bulb can be easily broken away. The bulbs are then stored in paper bags until fall, when they may be planted in the garden.

If your propagating frame is arranged so that you can maintain a constant temperature, or if you have some other means of doing so, there is another way of successfully forcing spring bulbs. We passed it by, because we found the method we have outlined so successful and simple that we did not need to use it. Like so many of our experiments in gardening under lights, this alternate method was first brought to our attention by a pamphlet published by the United States Department of Agriculture (*House Plants Bulletin No. 82*). We used a friend's controlled-temperature propagating frame and were pleased with the results. The bulbs are not planted, but stored dry at specific temperatures. Then they are planted and allowed to grow at 50 to 55 degrees Fahrenheit until the tip of the bulb is 1½ inches above the ground. After this, they are put under lights and blossom. Narcissus bulbs are stored for 12 weeks at 50 degrees; tulip bulbs at 45 degrees for 12 weeks, and hyacinth bulbs at 63 degrees for 4 weeks.

The important thing to remember in forcing any kind of bulb is to keep it growing at a temperature of about 50 degrees until you are ready to have it flower.

❋ *Varieties*

You will, of course, ask, "What varieties shall I grow?" For tulips you should choose the early singles, because the flower stems are rarely over fourteen inches tall. They have the added virtue that all bulbs planted in the same pot invariably bloom at the same time. Other varieties are not so obliging.

You have a wide choice among them. Pelican and White Hawk are good whites; Brilliant Scarlet and Colour Cardinal are excellent reds. Fred Moore and Prince of Austria are both fragrant and orange-red in color. But the early single we like most is General DeWett. It blooms even when mistreated. It is a beautiful orange, and, when planted in the garden after forcing, persists for many, many years. Carrar, a cottage tulip, forces nearly as easily as White Hawk, and has the same beautiful cuplike shape.

Two varieties of hyacinths can be forced much more easily than any of the others: L'Innocence, a large white; and Grand Maître, a pale blue. Both have strong, erect stems and beautiful leaves. There are a number of others which will grow nearly as easily under artificial lighting, but they are not as foolproof. King of the Blues, a dark blue; Lady Derby, a delicate pink with an intense fragrance; and Queen of the Yellows will blossom and give you variety in colors.

Two old-time favorites, one a daffodil, King Alfred, and the other a narcissus, Sir Watkins, force exceptionally well. They bloom early in the season, too, but they are not as long-lasting as the *Narcissus poeticus.* In this group, Lawrence Koster and Helios are both excellent for forcing. These are always delightful because of the many blossoms on each stem and their delicate fragrance.

And last, but far from least, is the *N. polyanthus,* familiarly called the paper-white. This is grown extensively in pebbles and water, together with its yellow-petaled sister Soleil d'Or. When the bulbs are planted in soil and grown under a tungsten or fluorescent lamp, they quite change their identity. These, of course, should not be put in cold storage; one needs only a cool temperature (45 to 55 degrees Fahrenheit) in order to have the roots develop normally; total darkness while the stems and flowers are pushing out of the bulbs proves to be a veritable fairy wand to the blossoms. By planting a few of these bulbs at twelve-day intervals from the middle of December, you can actually have spring-flowering plants for a large part of the year.

❀ ✳ ❦ ❋ ✿ ✳ *33*

FOLIAGE PLANTS

We studied the needs of foliage plants under artificial lights as carefully as we did those of plants that flower, but, as you might suspect, foliage plants are not as demanding. The very fact that for centuries some of them have been grown on windowsills shows a toughness to surrounding conditions that flowering plants seldom evidence. This very feature, combined with their interesting foliage, has made them houseplants. The foliage may be colored, dainty, or bold, as long as it is striking in some way. Their flowers are not spectacular enough, or sufficiently durable, to be centers of interest.

Many will survive for long intervals of time under a light intensity that measures from 15 to 35 foot-candles, the amount of light that comes through many windows in winter, but they can scarcely be called objects of beauty. Stems are weak and wispy and leaves are sparse. As artificial light is added they begin to grow more normally. Tables have been compiled to show the approximate amount of light various houseplants require. Many plants, such as the aspidistra, the dracaena, the philodendron, and the sansevieria, have long been grown because they can endure semidarkness. A new era dawns for them when you give them a light intensity that ranges from 125 to 250 foot-candles. They gallop ahead so spectacularly under these conditions that you will scarcely recognize them. It seems quite miraculous that such a small amount of additional light will cause such a transformation.

✽ Coleus

The coleus undergoes a complete metamorphosis under artificial light. On the windowsill its leaves are not especially big, nor are its colors strikingly bright. Under a light intensity of 500 to 1000 foot-candles it develops hues of red, yellow, orange, light brown, and dark brown nearly equaling its colors in the garden. You can grow coleus plants easily from a package of seeds. Start them for your garden in April, and for your indoor greenhouse in October.

✽ Ferns

Ferns, too, take on a new look, as soon as they are given the benefit of artificial light and the humidity of an enclosed case. The Boston fern, *Nephrolepsis bostoniensis,* probably the most popular of indoor ferns, under lights produces fronds that are nearly thirty inches long, within a few months' time. It takes on such majesty that you can easily understand why, for nearly three generations, it has held high honors in spite of its giantlike qualities. These pose problems in most apartments—problems which are magnified in a 4-by-6-foot indoor greenhouse.

Fortunately, sports have been developed from the Boston fern, which are smaller and more adaptable. A "sport" is the name given to an offspring from a parent plant which has different characteristics. These deviates of the Boston fern have many names, and new ones are still being developed.

Two of these ferns that we especially like are *Nephrolepsis veronica carigii* and *N. superbissima.* As one hesitates to mention varieties of African violets because all are so beautiful, so it is with these lacy ferns. Few of these last long on the windowsill, but they will grow anywhere about the house under tungsten or fluorescent lamps. Combined with the most prosaic of houseplants, they add grace and charm

to any planter arrangement. They have an added advantage of seem-
ing to be quite impervious to the presence of small traces of unconsumed gas.

We grow five ferns that are not of the Boston family, partly for
their beauty and partly as conversation pieces. These are best given a
good start under ample lighting, after which they will grow for considerable periods of time under a tungsten lamp, a fluorescent tube, or
even on the windowsill. When they droop you can rush them back to
your indoor greenhouse for two months of rejuvenation, and then
return them to their appointed household stations.

The first of these, *Asplenium nidus*, scarcely looks like a fern because its fronds are not divided. They are strongly veined and colored
a delicate light green that is quite translucent. It is commonly called
the bird's-nest fern, because the leaves start in a circle from the base to
form a perfect round nest. We are especially fond of it when it is
young and its fronds are not more than 4 or 5 inches tall. It is not such
a handsome plant when it reaches maturity, with its stiff fronds
18 to 20 inches long. It will grow well with 500 foot-candles of light.

Then there is the spleenwort, *Asplenium bulbiferum*, which so resembles the leaf of the carrot that our friends often accuse us of planting vegetables among our houseplants. Soon small bulblets appear on
the fronds, and new plants are formed. The resulting lacy fern has our
friends begging for bulblets so that they too may grow a "carrot."

These bulblets will not root unless they are sufficiently mature, so
that they almost separate themselves from the parent leaf. They are
then placed under lights (250 to 500 foot-candles) in a shallow dish in
which there is about ¼ inch of water. A soup bowl or a glass jar is
better than a saucer because the water does not evaporate so quickly.
The supply should be kept nearly constant at a depth of ⅛ to ¼ inch.
A few of the leaves will be submerged, but this does no harm. They
will root in two or three weeks. When we tried rooting them in vermiculite they took several months and fewer survived.

The third fern, which is quite different, is the holly fern, *Cyrto-
mium falcatum*. This one used to delight our children when they were
struggling with arithmetic, because of the mathematical precision with
which its leaves increase in length. Each new frond grows an addi-

tional pair of leaves—three, five, seven, and so on. Shape, texture, and contour of the leaflets remind you immediately of holly. An intensity of 500 to 750 foot-candles is best.

Another fern that occasions comment is known to the layman as the squirrel fern or the rabbit's-foot fern according to his own animal association, but to the horticulturist as *Polypodium aureum.* It throws out many brown, broad rhizomelike runners, which quite cover the pot in which it is growing and look (to us) not like a rabbit's foot or a brown squirrel's tail, but like an artistic jardiniere that the plant weaves for itself. Its fronds are so lacy that they are sufficient to establish the claims of this fern to beauty. It likes a very humid atmosphere, in which it will grow luxuriantly. On the edge of the fountain in our hall garden it grows under a 350-watt incandescent bulb. Without humidity it needs more light and does not grow as well.

Pteris ferns, too, are pleasant to grow, but they are harder to handle, for they will die immediately if you let them dry out. Their fronds are attractive and varied, and they are small in size. Under artificial lights, you can grow a table piece of them within a few weeks. It dies down at the end of its growth period. Pteris ferns are said to grow again after a resting period, but we so often forget to water them that we have never witnessed such a resurrection. Besides, it is always easier to grow new ones. Small plants are readily available and grow rapidly.

❁ *Ivies and Vines*

If you like to collect groups of things, you can also specialize in ivies. You will be surprised at how many varieties you can find. A friend of ours had a hundred and twenty-nine growing under a fluorescent fixture in her bedroom. They grow rapidly under artificial lights. Some become bushy plants, others trail. Lucile had grown them for a long time in a bay window, but she found that lamplight gave her much lovelier specimens. Until we saw Lucile's collection, we never dreamed there were so many hybrids.

Of the original English ivies, Hahn's branching ivy (*Hedera helix*) is one of the earlier ones, and still among the loveliest. It has small leaves and branches. There is an amusing one called twist-a-curl, which really does twist and curl as it trails, and a beautiful one from California called the crested ivy.

Then there is the Sylvanian ivy (*H. h. pedata*). It has the virtues of its other branching sisters, and also grows very fast, especially under artificial lights. We found that in a year's time three cuttings in a 3-inch pot developed into fifteen branching stems, a goodly number of them 24 inches long.

Another miniature, *H. h. miniatura variegata*, is interesting. Its white-edged leaves turn red in protest if conditions are not to its liking. If the red flag brings relief—sometimes more light, sometimes better soil—the color vanishes; otherwise it remains pink-leafed and refuses sulkily to grow.

Whether you decide to collect ivies or not, you will want to grow them. You can't keep house without an ivy: ivies in pots, ivies in glass bowls, ivies under lights, branching and creeping and producing so many leaves that they quite transform the corners of your indoor greenhouse with their profusion.

The grape ivy (*Cissus rhombifolia*) hails from an entirely different family, but it responds to artificial lighting in true ivy fashion, developing with speed and grace. Usually it is one of the most vigorous of houseplants and will grow under adverse circumstances.

The vigor of a cutting is especially dependent on the condition of the mother plant. A healthy, branching plant will give cuttings that root in a short time and grow vigorously. Cuttings from other plants behave like problem children. They root slowly and, when transplanted, their leaves fall. Grape ivy has a strong aversion to too much peat moss. Keeping this down to a minimum in a soil mixture promotes continued growth. Neither will the grape ivy stand the slightest amount of acid in the soil; it promptly curls up its leaves at a reading of pH 6.5. Small plants also die if placed in pots too large for them. Pay attention to these details, and grape ivy will grow almost anywhere. In a hanging basket, with only window light, one of ours grew so vigorously that it completely covered the upper and lower panes of glass. The fact that it was hanging over a radiator, protected by a cover, seemed to bother it not at all.

The wandering Jew (*Tradescantia fluminensis*) is almost as familiar a trailer as the ivy. It and a related species, *Zebrina pendula*, whose leaves are red and silver, root under artificial lights almost at the blinking of an eye. The variegated species, in protest against too much light, becomes completely yellow. Placed in darker quarters, it recovers its natural green and white.

One of our cuttings held an all-time record for fast rooting under lights. It grew a root in four hours. *Tradescantia* is also adept at producing a thick mass of trailing stems and blossoms. We had planted several varieties in the same pot. After a start under artificial lights, they grew in our living room from mantelpiece to floor, a beautiful tangle of green and yellow, red and silver, and solid greens. Traces of unconsumed gas fumes turn the leaves brown.

The philodendron earns its popularity because it is agreeable, come what may. Without strong likes or dislikes, it adjusts to home conditions. One summer we forgot a pot and left it for three months on a windowsill in a closed house. It was watered but once, when one of the children happened to stop at the house and, wondering what experiment Dad was trying now, soaked it with water. Contrary to all the rules, it lived the summer through and continued to flourish the next winter.

Philodendrons have shown their stamina in other ways. We needed a plant to grow on a wall-bracket, so we picked one that had grown husky under artificial lights. Against the ivory wall its long, hanging tendrils made a pattern of green which scarcely changed in the three months we left it there. Any other plant would have lost its leaves within two weeks, as the light intensity varied between 20 and 35 foot-candles.

Like all our other foliage plants, it never failed to respond with thick stems and many leaves when placed under lights. Plants with wispy stems do not suddenly become sturdier; they need help. The tip of each stem should be buried in the earth of the pot. It will push through, and come up much thicker. Sometimes it must be buried two or three times to produce a truly husky stem. Of course, you do not cut the tip off the plant in the process; you just enable it to rejuvenate itself, for only thick stems produce large, healthy leaves.

The large-leafed philodendron (*Philodendron massive*) is a bigger edition of the small-sized variety. It, too, is a vine, and its glossy leaves are from nine to twelve inches long. Under lamps a cutting grows into a plant eighteen inches tall in three months. By the end of a year it will have become so big and leggy that you will, no doubt, want to start it anew. You need only to cut off the stem and root it.

Another member of the species, the cut-leaf philodendron, when young, looks like a bouquet of leaves—each leaf deeply serrated, like an oak leaf. Like the large-leafed philodendron, it quickly becomes a trailer, and, along with the other members of its family, can grow where little light is available. It is more attractive when trained to climb rather than to trail. On a totem pole, the cut-leaf philodendron makes a particularly handsome plant, although any of the philodendrons may be used. Select a pole three to five times taller than the container in which the totem is to be used. Wrap the pole with a layer of sphagnum moss 2 to 3 inches deep. Hold it in place with string. Push the pole into the soil and wrap the philodendron around it, holding it in place with hairpins. It is important to keep the moss damp so that the roots will grow into the moss and the leaves will form a solid mass. We have found these philodendron totem poles make delightful gifts, and under lights the plants grow very fast.

❁ *Plants Best Grown as Babies*

Dieffenbachia. Other plants besides the large-leafed philodendron are useful only as babies. A number of these will grow in light intensities that are quite low. One of these is the *Dieffenbachia*, which responds quickly to a tungsten bulb or a fluorescent tube. For us it early acquired a sentimental significance. This erect-growing plant, which shoots up so fast under artificial lights, endeared itself to us not because of its mottled, spotted, or striped foliage, but because it was the first plant our youngest son recognized. He rolled off its many syllables with facility, to his own and his parents' delight. How glad we were that he said "dieffenbachia," and not "dumb cane," as it is popularly called. It gains this name through its ability to make you temporarily speechless if you chew the stem of one of its species. There are several varieties with different types of leaves. The leaves of one type, *D. picta*, have numerous oblong and linear spots along the veins, which combine to make interesting patterns. Spots and stripes are the rule with *D. seguine*, but with a different effect, for the stripes predominate. The leaves of *D. splendens* are mottled light and dark green. Until they reach a height of a foot, the stems keep their leaves. After this the bottom ones begin to drop off. When this happens, cut off the tops of these plants. Put them under the lights, and they will soon root again. By this means you can keep dieffenbachia always young, useful, and attractive.

Dracaena. Dracaenas, like dieffenbachias, are charming when young and intolerable when old. They too lose their bottom leaves, and as they grow tall they come to resemble inverted feather dusters, with straplike leaves coming out of their sheathed stems. We grew one in our living room until the top touched the ceiling, interesting enough from the scientific point of view, but scarcely so from the pictorial angle. In its first year of growth you would never suspect that it had such gangling possibilities. Striped green-and-yellow leaves, or, as with *Dracaena sanderiana*, green ones edged with white, come out and bend back upon themselves like plumes of a little green fountain. It is a strictly formal plant, but entirely delightful. You will want to grow it in pairs, or singly as the proper focal point of any triangular arrangement. *D. sanderiana* is by far the most common of the many species of dracaena, possibly because it withstands almost any abuse. But there are two others that are worth seeking out because of their interesting leaves and growth. The zebra plant, *D. goldieana*, is a native of Africa. If any plant can remind you of a zebra, this one does. You can see its decorative possibilities. Another dracaena, *D. godseffiana*, is always worth growing. Some of its leaves grow in whorls, while others are erect and straight. The varied combinations of lines make it an unusual and interesting plant.

Screw pine. The screw pine, or pandanus, is an attractive youngster and a vicious oldster. Its striped green-and-white leaves make a formal symmetry which is even more delicate and pleasing than that of the dracaena. Until the pandanus is a foot or a foot and a half tall, it is a picture of grace. As it grows, the dainty, picoted edges of the leaves develop into spiny prickles which jab anyone who comes near —even though one has the kindly purpose of watering it. This makes one feel it is a "bad plant," scarcely worth growing even as a scientific curiosity. As soon as it matures enough to grow taller, it sends out roots from farther and farther up the stem, giving the effect of a plant standing on stilts. It grows fast under lights and can soon be moved to the windowsill. It will grow even on a radiator cover.

Mexican Bread Plant (*Monstera deliciosa*). In many arrangements, you will want plants that grow tall. By carefully training the large-leafed, rambling, rapid-growing monstera, you can have both height and symmetry. Since its leaves are divided into segments, this plant has a decorative boldness in its blending of light and shadow. The leaves are mammoth in size. By means of lights and judicious tying, you can quickly produce plants that are from two to four feet tall. Monstera roots from a cutting, but the first few leaves that develop are not divided. In six months, under artificial lights, you can grow a plant that is larger than the dracaena would be in two years. Of course, since it grows so vigorously, you must fertilize it often and regularly.

❀ Hanging-Basket Plants

Strawberry Geranium. The strawberry geranium (*Saxifraga sarmentosa*), when well grown, is almost a perfect colonial bouquet. From the center of the plant, spikes of foamy flowers arise surrounded by a symmetrical circle of leaves. The leaves are dark green, hairy, lightly penciled at the veins, beautifully scalloped, and flecked underneath with red. To complete the composition, bright red runners start from the center of the plant, grow over the edges of the pot, and sprout tiny plants at their tips.

Small wonder that our grandmothers loved it. But it is rarely grown today, not so much from lack of desire but because it is so often pest-infected. Not knowing the reason for its poor showing, home gardeners often discard the plant without ever appreciating its full beauty.

Flowers, unfortunately, are not common. They never appear in a cycle of 18 hours of lamplight and 6 of darkness. To form, they need a two-month period in a cool greenhouse with a cycle of 10 hours of lamplight. When the buds have formed, the cycle or the light intensity does not matter.

Spider Lily. The spider lily (*Chlorophytum elatum variegatum*) also sends out runners. Actually these are flower stems, but the white-petaled flowers are fleeting and insignificant. Small plantlets develop from the blossoms. Of the several varieties, beware of the long-leafed green plant which sends out flower stems three or four feet long with wispy plants at their ends. It looks for all the world like a large spider dangling on its web. Choose the variegated plant of the species, which has short streamers that make an attractive outline without the spider-like appearance; you may prefer to call it by its other name, the St. Bernard lily. Under artificial lights four flower stems develop for every one that appears on the windowsill. It takes about three months under lights to grow a picture plant, one that has from twelve to sixteen streamers, each bearing a flourishing plant.

Water it every day. The spider lily will survive considerable neglect because it develops its own storage tanks, large underground tubers for holding water; but daily watering increases its beauty. It will grow when you give it only 8 or 10 hours of light, but it likes a light intensity of 250 to 500 foot-candles and a longer cycle.

❀ *Foliage Plants for Emphasis*

The Fan Plant. The fan plant (*Marica gracilis*) resembles the iris of the garden. Its striking decorative feature is the manner in which its leaves grow; they form a perfect fan. Usually twelve leaves occur in each fan, which is why some people call it the apostle plant. Other shoots may develop from the same roots, but each group has its distinctive fan shape.

Under artificial lights, it blossoms quickly. Its irislike flower, which grows a little awkwardly from one side of a leaf, is exquisite but transitory, lasting only one day—just an extra dividend on a plant whose stiff but attractive foliage serves as a focal point in many arrangements.

The Prayer Plant. The prayer plant (*Maranta leuconeura*) roots easily from a shoot in about ten days under artificial lights. It grows so rapidly that in four to six months it completely fills a 5-inch pot. It gains its name from the fact that every evening it folds its leaves together. The fact that puzzled us the most was that under a light intensity of 450 foot-candles it would still fold its leaves together as soon as it was dark outside. Our indoor greenhouse is by a window, but the window light intensity, in the winter months, measures only 10 foot-candles. We continually asked ourselves whether the lack of those few rays of natural light was all the maranta needed to make it "fold its hands in prayer."

The Piggy-Back Plant. The piggy-back plant (*Tolmiea menzie-seii*) is a boon to those who have slight traces of unconsumed gas in their homes, about which little can be done. Fumes have little effect on the robust piggy-back plant. A new little plant forms rapidly on each leaf, giving the plant its name. Dour people, who find other uses for their backs than hauling children around, call it the pick-a-back plant. The many little plants give the mother plant a fluffy and bushy look, which makes the plant useful for emphasis.

Peperomia. Several peperomias grow easily in the house and beautifully under artificial lights. The watermelon begonia, *Peperomia sandersii argyreia*, is one worth growing for its leaves, which are dark green with silvery or yellowish-white streaks. The color sense of the individuals who describe it seems to differ, but you will instantly recognize it, for the markings on the leaves remind you exactly of the markings on an early summer watermelon. The fact that the heart-shaped leaves are attached to the bright red stems at almost right angles makes for a definite variety of line. Its sister, *P. arifolia*, will grow or, more accurately, stand still in the darkest of places. Even under artificial lights it is a slow grower, but attractive, with its succulent, thick, green leaves splotched with yellow. To grow luxuriantly it needs 1000 foot-candles.

But the most delightful of all peperomias is not as common as these two. It is the *P. nunularifolia*, a delicate creeper with threadlike stems thickly covered with small leaves, which are almost round except for the pointed ones at the tips of the stems. It reminds you of baby's-tears (*Helxine soleirolii*). It likes moisture, like the baby's-tears, but it does not brown off if you forget to water it. It grows sturdily on the windowsill and is almost weedlike under artificial lights. Its tender leaves hang tremulously on long, slender stems, and sometimes, like water drops, they reflect enough light to give the plant a whitish or silvery cast.

Stingless Nettle. The stingless nettle (*Pilea pumila*) is another plant that should have wider recognition, for it is so attractive and grows and branches with vigor under artificial lights. Its tiny blossoms, so small that they look like masses of tiny drops viewed under the microscope, are dainty enough for a fairy-queen's bonnet. They last a long time, and when they vanish, new branches start to grow. The leaves are quilted and a dark reddish-green. The stingless nettle deserves a better name, and a place in the home among other colored-leaf plants.

The Chinese Evergreen. The Chinese evergreen (*Aglaonema pictum*) is familiar to most houseplant lovers, for it takes abuse without losing a leaf. It will grow in water; but in soil, under lamplight, it flourishes. We had one which quickly outgrew our greenhouse, so we gave it to a friend. When we saw it several years later the plant was huge and strangely interesting. It gained its decorative value not so much from the leaves, but from the outline made by its shaggy, hemplike stem. Even its jack-in-the-pulpitlike flowers stood out appealingly. A variegated form, *A. costatum*, is prettier but does not grow as fast.

African Evergreen. The African evergreen (*Nephthytis afzelii*), like the Chinese evergreen, is hardy and will also grow in water. Its arrow-shaped, glossy leaves make a more interesting pattern than do those of the Chinese evergreen. It too grows better when in good soil. The best variety is *N. triphylla*. Its yellowish-white-and-green leaves divide into three parts, giving a flowerlike effect. A leaf from this plant looks like three leaves, but it is held together at the base of the center section with a heavy vein. The plant is especially lovely under artificial lights, where the green becomes rich and dark, and the light markings provide a contrast of almost pure white.

❀ Holly

Everyone loves holly at Christmastime with its beautiful shiny leaves and red berries. Those who grow it successfully under lights love it the whole year through. Holly will grow best in a light intensity of from 1400 to 2500 foot-candles; it will grow with less light, however, but it won't produce as much fruit. In order to have berries, of course you will need the female plant, and you will be sure of getting that by rooting cuttings.

We usually plant cuttings from various hollies in perlite although a combination of perlite and sphagnum moss has also proved effective, as we discovered in rooting the Japanese holly *Ilex crenata*. We use bottom heat to keep the temperature of the rooting medium at 70 degrees Fahrenheit.

The United States Department of Agriculture at its Beltsville, Maryland, station has found that a long day of 16 to 18 hours is essential to holly-rooting. By shutting off the light briefly and interrupting the long day to create the effect of two short nights, scientists discovered that the plants responded with earlier and heavier rooting. The light-interruption also stimulated bud break and the growth of some of the clones. Although the same effect is achieved by a full 18-hour day and 6-hour night, interrupting the night apparently speeds up the process. *Ilex cenata* was the most responsive of the hollies. Others, however, responded favorably; among them were *Ilex taxa, I. aquifolium, I. cornuta, I. pedunculosa,* and *I. pernyi.*

We have named only a few of the plants you can grow under artificial lights, but the opportunity for experiment is one of the most pleasant offshoots of this hobby. If we have led you at least to the flower-strewn path of the indoor gardener, we shall have achieved our major purpose and you will find your way from there. But if you grow only the flowers listed here, or even half of them, your house will radiate the joy of living things.

❀ ✳ ❦ ✾ ❀ ✳ *34*

PLANTS TO MEET
A NEED

A sure way of having beautiful plants is to fit the plants to the people.
It is as important as fitting the lights to the plants. There are plants for
the business man and woman, for the avid gardener, for those who
wish they were gardeners, for students, for the professional decorator,
for those who want friends, for homemakers, for children. There is a
plant to meet each need. You'll have more fun and greater success, if
you grow *your* kind of plant. Thanks to the availability of artificial
lights, it's possible to take such a psychological approach.

If you have not grown many plants, or are not familiar with how
much light *your* kind of plant may require, the lists that follow should
be helpful. Many of them have been mentioned, but grouping them
can help you in choosing the right plants for your indoor gardens, for
your office, for public buildings, for traditional and modern interiors.
Most of all it should encourage you to make your own lists for your
own indoor gardens, just as you do for those out of doors.

❀ *Plants That Will Give You Friends*

African violets, begonias, gesneriads, orchids. (These require from
600 to 1500 foot-candles, depending on the species and variety.)

These plants open the door for a common meeting with others who grow them. There is an African Violet Society, a Begonia Society, an American Gloxinia and Gesneriad Society, the American Orchid Society, and even an Indoor Light Gardening Society. Many publish helpful bulletins for their members.

✽ Plants for Children

Every child should have his own plant. It opens new horizons, encourages the discipline of caring for a plant. Any of the hard-to-kill plants from the list for public buildings below could be used, but plants that do things are more interesting. The artillery plant (*Pilea microphylla*) gains its name because the flowers discharge a cloud of pollen when shaken (650 foot-candles). Its small, compact, fernlike leaves are also decorative. The prayer plant (*Maranta leuconeura*) folds its leaves in prayer every night (150 to 250 foot-candles). Sorrel (*Rumex*), usually thought of as a weed, also closes its leaves at night. In many parts of the world, sorrel leaves are gathered as pot herbs, and we have used them with good results in soups and salads. They are so easily grown from seed that a child can watch the entire growing process. Sorrel grows rapidly under 250 foot-candles of light, but it will grow under 35 foot-candles. The piggy-back plant is easily grown and is another favorite (50 foot-candles and up).

✽ Plants for the Radiator

The bane of plants is too much heat, and so often in a window where there is excellent light, there is also a radiator. We grew a number of plants on our radiator, which was protected with a radiator cover. When we added lights to the window, and a galvanized tray enclosed in wood, some of the plants blossomed. We filled the tray with ½ inch of pebbles and water. Even without this added effort, three came through with flying colors: the screw pine (*Pandanus veitchii*), the *Dracaena sanderiana*, and the familiar *Sansevieria trifasciata*. The latter grew so well that a nongardening friend thought it was an orchid plant that was not in flower.

❀ Plants for Public Buildings

These plants are of course equally good for the home, the would-be gardener, and the office. They will grow in a light intensity of 100 foot-candles, and do very well indeed if given as high an intensity as 250 foot-candles. The dieffenbachias are among the more spectacular foliage plants with their dark green leaves and white markings. *Dieffenbachia amoena* has markings on the veins; *D. Rudolph Roehrs* has yellow-green leaves that are blotched with yellow and edged with green. In a small "composition," dieffenbachias can take the place of flowers under 250 foot-candles. Three plants that can be grouped together under 250 foot-candles and spotlighted with an incandescent lamp are the Norfolk pine (*Araucaria excelsa*), the *Pilea caderei*, which has attractive variegated green-and-white leaves, and the *Rhoeo discolor*, sometimes called Moses in the bulrushes.

Another combination that is unusual and looks well in a group because of the different shapes of the leaves are the snake plant, the rubber plant, and the croton. The leaves of the croton are variously shaped and marked with patterns of yellow, scarlet, and green. You cannot use the croton, however, unless you have a good light intensity of 750 to 1000 foot-candles and constant moisture. Lacking this you can substitute a bromeliad, and use 250 foot-candles of lights.

Bromeliads, any varieties that you can find, are worth growing in groups in offices, public buildings, and homes. If the centers can be kept full of water and the light intensity increased, you are rewarded with spectacular flowers. Under three 150-watt incandescent lamps you can grow a rubber tree to almost any height. You can put with it the large-leafed philodendron, and the yew podocarpus. Like the rubber plant, yew will grow very tall, but its height is not usually fulfilled in dim light of 250 foot-candles. Much better is a light intensity of 750 foot-candles.

❀ Hard-to-Kill Plants

These are the plants for those of you who really want a "bit of green" and not too much work. If you water twice a week and give them artificial light of 250 to 500 foot-candles, the amount that two 4-foot fluorescent lamps will give, you'll be called clever; and if you substitute Power-Groove tubes or Gro-lux for the fluorescent, you'll be called a gardener. Here are the easy plants:

Wandering Jews (*Zebrina pendula*, *Tradescantia fluminensis*, and *Commelina nudiflora*). They look like brothers in spite of their different names.

The *Syngonium*, more popularly known by florists as *Nephthytis*, has silver-white centers in heart-shaped leaves and grows easily.

The coleus will grow in water, though it does better in soil.

The Chinese evergreen (*Aglaonema*) grows in water or in a dark spot with almost no care at all.

✿ Market-Basket Plants

If you are thrifty and would like some houseplants as a by-product of your market basket, you can grow some attractive plants under a light intensity of 1000 to 1500 foot-candles. Grapefruit seed planted in a pan-sized pot makes an effective plant. The avocado plant will grow four feet high and eventually outgrow the greenhouse. It will languish if it does not have a sunny window. Orange and lemon seeds will grow in the house, but you cannot be sure that they will bear fruit, though some orange seeds blossomed for us under lights. Those that are most likely to fruit are the Otaheite orange, the ponderosa lemon, and the Meyer lemon.

✿ Challenging Plants

If you want to grow plants that are really a challenge, you might try the camellia and the gardenia—such lovely plants and so hard to grow. Yet it can be done, as Rey Wesley, one of our correspondents, proved in Park Forest, Illinois.

"I'm quite sure that the most significant ingredients in my gardenia growing have been affection and persistence. For success there must be a humid atmosphere and the soil must be acid. We have a very large picture window facing east. My gardenia flowered profusely in midsummer out of doors, and again late in September it was heavily budded. It had grown so big in the garden that I had no pot to accommodate it. So I punched holes in the bottom of an old scrub bucket, laid a few layers of gravel and peat moss in the bottom, and dug up the plant and brought it indoors. It sat on an old rubber sink drain with two coffee cans of water beneath the foliage, under fluorescent lamps and the light from the picture window (a total of 1000 to 1500 foot-candles). Not only did all the buds bloom, but a few new ones formed and bloomed sporadically throughout the winter. The plant now has progeny, some with friends, one in my office window, and all in bud."

GROWING
PRIZE-WINNING PLANTS

You will not have grown plants under lights for more than a few months before you begin to think to yourself that they are the best-looking plants you have ever seen. "They'd win in a flower show," you say. As the months pass, your pride in them grows. "I might enter them in the next garden club show," you think.

It's not so much a sense of competition that makes most of us enter a flower show as it is the tangible proof of success that comes with a blue ribbon or a silver cup. That brief moment of triumph, however, has taken long hours of preparation. If you are interested in winning prizes with plants, you have a powerful ally in artificial lights. Properly used, they can make even a wispy flower into a prima donna.

We can still remember our first entry in the International Flower Show in New York City. As we took our plants out of their warm coverings, we heard someone exclaim, "Some greenhouse!" Yet the possibilities of artificial light were so little understood then that neither the speaker nor the judges could believe they had been grown exclusively under lights.

For three or more years we entered plants in the International Flower Show. Each year the plants won firsts in the class in which they were entered. One gesneriad, *Tula flava*, won the purple ribbon, an award given only to plants of outstanding distinction.

Actually there is no wonder in the accomplishment. It serves to demonstrate the fact that where conditions for plant growth can be completely controlled, perfect plants can be grown. Our prize-winners came from cases in which coolwhite fluorescent tubes were combined with incandescent bulbs in a ratio of 3 to 1. They had the plush abundant look of plants that have enough light to meet their needs. Of course, their other needs were cared for as well. The best garden site in the world needs care. We had not been to our summer home for three years and the gardens were overgrown. A friend knowing our interest in gardens stopped to admire. "What a tremendous leaf you have," she said. "Is that what they call elephant ears?" It was difficult to tell her it was a burdock.

Prize-winning plants must have the right soil, the right care, the benevolence of the right lights, and love. And yet, there was the orchid *Odontoglossum citrosmum*. Frederick was ready to throw it out because, although it was a beautiful specimen, nothing he did would make it flower. I rescued it and put it in a cool upstairs bedroom on the windowsill. Out of sight, it was more or less out of mind. It spent the winter there, sometimes being watered, sometimes not, until one day in April, when we happened to go into the room together. The plant was covered with long strings of artificial flowers.

We laughed, the children had been playing tricks on us. We walked over to look at the plant more closely. The flowers were not artificial, they were *real*! It was the most outstanding orchid we had ever flowered. Of course, we took credit for it unabashedly, and gaily sent it on its prize-winning way. The touch of gall in our cup was that we never succeeded in doing it again, regardless of the treatment: love, neglect, or a little of both.

You may have heard the theory that plants communicate. To quote Thorn Bacon in *National Wildlife*, "Staggering as it may be to contemplate, a life signal may connect all creation." His comment was based on the work that Cleve Backster is doing recording plant reactions with his lie-detector. By means of a psychogalvanic reflex electrode on each side of a leaf to bring it into balance, the stimulated plant exhibits a reaction pattern typical of a graph made by a human under emotional stimulation. By the right stimulation he could make the plant scream, in the language of the lie-detector!

Don't let your plants scream. You need to use that inner something that makes you look at plants with the same tenderness a mother has while looking at her children. You need balanced lighting that gives a light intensity of from 1000 to 1500 foot-candles. You need an enclosed indoor greenhouse. Careful thought must be given to the cultural directions given in this book. *They need to be followed accurately.*

Here are some simple rules that may be of help to you in growing prize-winning plants. Begin with what appear to be exceptional plants. You may buy fine varieties from growers, or you can select the best of your own seedlings. Often the seedlings that are first to germinate have the most vitality, but sometimes slow starters have the most exceptional characteristics. Watch for excellence. What you are seeking are the best bloomers, as well as plants that are symmetrical, well-proportioned, and compact. And of course the leaves must be perfect. There must be no pest damage, and leaves and flowers must form an attractive pattern. Perfect, abundant flowers are the key to a judge's heart. Only under lights do they open in such fullness, such petal-by-petal perfection.

Plants stay so beautiful under lights for such a long time that you should have no trouble having them in the best possible shape when the show opens. Have your plants clean, without a single poor leaf or a damaged flower. Label your plants intelligently with both the common and the scientific names.

Finally, be careful in transplanting them to the show. A friend of ours flew his plants to the International Flower Show and they froze because he let them be put in the baggage compartment of the airplane. Even if the show is just around the corner, getting them there is a problem. Pack them carefully with tissue paper, hold them in place in the cartons with newspapers. Carry them as though they were china. You don't want to fail on the last round. You can expect to win.

Appendices

LIGHT NEEDS OF PLANTS

IN INDOOR GARDENING

Most houseplants barely exist in a light intensity of 50 foot-candles; increasing it to 250 foot-candles transforms them into a luxuriant mass of foliage. In the second grouping, a light intensity between 250 and 650 foot-candles is the fairy godmother that makes ordinary houseplants (African violets, begonias, beloperone, and many others) blossom profusely; while the third category is the light intensity that gives you your heart's desire, a garden where you can grow orchids, garden flowers, and the so-called florist plants.

Plants Needing Light Intensity of 50 to 250 Foot-Candles

PLANT	COMMON NAME	NOTES
Aspidistra elatior	Cast-iron plant	Grows on windowsill with very little light, about 50 foot-candles
Aspidistra elatior variegata	Variegated cast-iron plant	Because of white areas on foliage, somewhat more light is needed
Agave americana	Century plant	Leaves stiff, recurve lined with sharp thorns; some

PLANT	COMMON NAME	NOTES
		people like them as small plants
Aucuba japonica	Gold-dust plant	Stiff, waxy foliage, blotched with yellow
Helxine soleirolii	Baby's-tears	Attractive if you keep it moist all the time
Piper nigrum	Pepper plant	This is the pepper plant of commerce, but grows in the house quite similarly to phil-odendron
Rhoeo discolor vittata	Oyster flower	Flowers are blended with the leaves and are borne in a small cup; underside of leaves is purple, and upper surface silver-green striped with yellow

Plants Needing Light Intensity of 250 to 650 Foot-Candles

PLANT	COMMON NAME	NOTES
Abutilon hybridum	Flowering maple	Attractive bell-shaped flow-ers; grow above 60 degrees Fahrenheit
Amaryllis hippeastrum vittatum	Amaryllis	Plant bulbs halfway in ground; blossoms well with 250 foot-candles; can be grown from bulbs or from seed
Euphorbia splendens	Crown-of-thorns	Coarse thorns completely cover stems; few leaves near tips; reddish-orange flowers
Oxalis	Bermuda buttercup	Bulbs planted in soil and placed under lights will flower in five to six months

PLANT	COMMON NAME	NOTES
Senecio mikanioides	German ivy	Makes an attractive, bushy, ivylike growth; if given short days for a month, with cool temperature, produces an abundance of yellow flowers in light intensities of 450 to 650 foot-candles

Plants Needing Light Intensity of 650 to 1400 Foot-Candles

If you give your plants an 18-hour day at this light intensity, they will grow in your own home during the winter months as well as they would in most commercial greenhouses. Annuals may be started for the garden, and many will blossom under the lights. Perennials may be started for the garden, and many can be grown to maturity, if desired. Most of the low-growing so-called florist plants may be grown in this light intensity. Notes on some of these plants follow.

PLANT	PROPAGATION	NOTES
Tuberous Begonia	Cuttings from garden plants; seeds	Seeds sown in mid-December will make blossoming plants for your garden in May; or seed may be sown early and plants flowered under lights
Christmas Cherry (*Solanum pseudo-capsicum*)	Seeds	Seeds may be sown in February, the plants grown in the garden during the summer, and brought back under the lights in the fall for plants at Christmas
Christmas Pepper (*Capsicum frutescens*)	Seeds	Grows faster than Christmas Cherry and does not lose its leaves as easily when brought indoors in the fall; is grown in same manner; sow in late March

PLANT	PROPAGATION	NOTES
Slipperwort (*Calceolaria*)	Seeds	Lovely pouch-shaped flowers in yellow, pink, red, and bronze; sow ten months before you want blooms
Panda Plant (*Kalanchoe*)	Seeds	Needs a short day for four weeks, at the beginning of the eighth month, in order to form buds; after that it can be given a longer day; blooms beautifully; takes ten months from seed to flower
Primrose (*Primula malacoides*) (The hybrids developed in California, *Primula* hybrid Pacific, are outstanding.)	Seeds	Keep at 50 degrees Fahrenheit at night; sow six months in advance of time you want bloom; provide constant moisture and short days for 1½ months before you expect flowers

I I

GUIDELINES FOR THE
GERMINATION OF SEEDS

Henry M. Cathey, United States Department of Agriculture

[The names of the flower seeds used in these tables were the special ones that Mr. Cathey used in his particular experiments, but they have a broad meaning. For example, in Group 1, White Ball Aster is listed. Other types of asters should be given the same treatment.

There are a number of plants where the Latin name has become the popular one. Some of the plants may be hard to find, but they can easily be grown from seed. Early Ball Myosotis is a good example. Any form of *Myosotis compacta*, with its numerous flowers, is a great addition to any garden.]

1. These seeds germinate over a wide temperature range without a light requirement: Golden Ageratum, Carpet of Snow Alyssum, White Ball Aster, Giant White Candytuft, Florist Mixture Clarkia, Purple Cup-and-Saucer Vine (*Cobaea*), Unwins Dwarf Mix Dahlia, Bravo Dianthus, Annual Poinsettia (*Euphorbia*), Covent Gypsophila, Bright Green Kochia, Doubloon Marigold, Spry Marigold, Early White Mignonette, Nudicaule Poppy, Iceberg Statice, Lavender Column Stock, Golden Standard Wallflower.

2. These seeds germinate only at cool temperatures (around 55 de-

grees Fahrenheit) without a light requirement: Radiance Cosmos, Orange/
Orange Improved Dimorphotheca, Sweet Marjoram.

3. These seeds germinate only at a warm temperature (around 75 de-
grees Fahrenheit), without a light requirement: Molten Fire Amaranthus,
Scarlet Balsam, Annual Mix Campanula, Toreador Celosia, Masterpiece
Christmas Cherry, Vivid Cineraria, Tetra Red Giant Gaillardia, *Gom-
phrena rubra*, Hunnemannia, Crystal Palace Lobelia, Heavenly Blue Morn-
ing Glory, Purple Robe Nierembergia, Single Gloriosa Daisy (*Rudbeckia*),
Emperor Mix Salpiglossis, Giant Blue Scabiosa, *Thunbergia gibsoni*,
Torenia, *Zinnia isabellina*.

4. These seeds germinate only at a restricted range of temperatures without a light requirement. Optimum temperatures are given.

55 degrees Fahrenheit: Giant King Lupine, Early Ball Myosotis, Ruth
Cuthbertson Sweet Pea.

60 degrees Fahrenheit: Chives (Grass Onion), Cynoglossum, Dill, Ga-
zania, Powderpuff Hollyhock, Perennial Rosemary.

65 degrees Fahrenheit: Sweet Fennel, White Giant Freesia, Golden
Giant Nasturtium.

70 degrees Fahrenheit: Anise, Chiband's Imperial Cardinal Red Carna-
tion, Marine Heliotrope, Yellow Portulaca.

75 degrees Fahrenheit: Blue Lace Didiscas, Blue Plumbago, Perennial
Thyme.

5. These seeds germinate over a wide temperature range when exposed
to light: Scandinavia Pink Fibrous-Root Begonia, Sapphire Browallia,
Tiddly-Winks Exacum, Gloxinia, Vulcan Kalanchoe, Art Shades Naegelia,
Blue Fairy Tale Saintpaulia, Streptocarpus (optimum temperature: 75
degrees Fahrenheit).

6. Germination for these seeds is enhanced over a wide temperature
range when exposed to light: Blue Mink Ageratum, Double Mix Tuberous-
Root Begonia, Blue Bells Browallia, *Calceolaria multiflora nana*; Firefly
Cuphea; Grevillea (Australian Silk Oak); *Impatiens holsti* Scarlet, Bur-
gundy Perilla, Maytime Petunia, *Primula malacoides* White Giant, Fas-
bender's Red Primula, St. John's Fire Salvia, Bohnenkraut Savory.

7. These seeds germinate over a wide temperature range but are en-
hanced at a warm temperature when exposed to light: *Cineraria maritima*
Diamond, Red Rainbow Coleus, Double White Imperial Ball Feverfew,
Helichrysum (Everlasting), Crimson Bedder Nicotiana, Orchid Rocket
Snapdragon.

8. These seeds germinate over a wide temperature range when held in
the dark: Borage, Orange Coronet Calendula, Blue Boy Centaurea, Yellow

Centaurea, Sensation Mixture Penstemon, Glamour Phlox, Giant Mix Ball Schizanthus, Smilax, *Statice suworowii* Russian, Torch Tithonia, White Vinca.

9. These seeds germinate over a wide temperature range but are enhanced at warm temperature when held in the dark: Pure White Cyclamen, White Supreme Larkspur, *Mesembryanthemum criniflorum*, Fire King Nemesia, Lake of Thun Pansy, Extra Triple Curled Parsley, True Irish Shamrock, Blue Elf Viola.

III

EXPERIMENTS

FOR HOME AND SCHOOL

In addition to the experiments described in the book, others are suggested here. Our ability to grow plants entirely with artificial lights is a new and only partially explored field, which makes it of great interest to the student-scientist. Supplementary help in planning experiments can be gained from Miscellaneous Publication No. 879, published by the United States Department of Agriculture: *Light and Plants* by R. J. Downs, H. A. Borthwick, and A. A. Piringer.

Experiments can be carried out with seeds to show that:

1. Certain kinds of seeds require light in order to germinate. (Experiment with different varieties, with seeds of different ages, etc.)

2. A light requirement can be induced in seeds that normally do not require light for germination.

3. The photoreaction that allows germination to proceed is reversible: red radiant energy will cause one reaction while far-red causes the opposite.

4. The sensitivity of seeds to a given amount of radiant energy changes with the period of inhibition.

See also the section entitled "Testing Your Seeds" in Chapter 22.

The effects of light on plant growth can be experimented with to show how:

1. Light inhibits stem growth and promotes leaf expansion.
2. Plants bend toward the light.
3. Chlorophyll formation requires light, and the light must be of a higher intensity than that which controls stem length.
4. The red/far-red reversible photoreaction that controls seed germination also controls stem length and leaf size.

See also Chapter 2 for the experiment with different kinds of light.

Many interesting aspects of photoperiodism can be demonstrated:

1. What varieties of plants flower on short days and long nights? On long days and short nights?
2. What seeds that seem to need a lot of light to germinate will have the same result with a few minutes' exposure every hour for 12 hours? (*Puya berteronia*, a bromeliad, is one example. Although it is more practical for the home gardener to give it continuous light for 8 or 10 hours, only a few minutes every hour for half a day will cause the seeds to germinate 100 per cent.)
3. Demonstrate that the dormancy of woody plants in the autumn can be brought about by short days.
4. Demonstrate that the length of the day controls tuber- and bulb-formation as well as flowering and dormancy.

Since almost all of these experiments can be carried out with two fluorescent coolwhite 40-watt tubes with the plants approximately 2 inches below them (never more than 1 foot), it is possible for the biology student to perform these experiments either at home or in the schoolroom.

IV

SUGGESTIONS FOR

FURTHER READING

United States Department of Agriculture Publications

Cathey, Henry M., *Photobiology in Horticulture.*
Downs, R. J., H. A. Borthwick, and A. A. Piringer, *Light and Plants.*
Indoor Gardens for Decorative Plants (Home and Garden Bulletin 133).
Lane, H. C., H. M. McCarthy, and I. T. Evans, *The Dependence of Flowering in Several Long-Day Plants on the Spectral Composition of Light Extending the Photoperiod.*
Light Sources Used in Horticulture in the U.S.A.
Piringer, A. A., *Photoperiod, Supplemental Light, and Rooting of Cuttings.*
Plant Propagation with Artificial Light (CA-34-76).

Cooperative Extension Service, New York State
College of Agriculture at Cornell University

A Guide to Safe Pest Control around the Home (No. 74).

General Electric Company Lamp Division, Cleveland, Ohio

Ditchman, J. P., *Light for Plant Growth.*
Fluorescent Lamps.
High Intensity Discharge Lamps.

Outdoor Lighting for Family Living (LS-171 R).
Plant Growth Lighting (TP 127).

Sylvania Lighting Campany

Cyclic Lighting for Plant Growth (Bulletin 231).
The Gro-Lux Lamp.
Gro-Lux Wide Spectrum Fluorescent Lamp (O-294).
Orchid Growth with the Gro-Lux Fluorescent Lamp (O-286).

INDEX